Roberta Matuson has good news: you don't have to be born with personal magnetism to be a great leader. With her guidance, you can learn to be irresistibly, magnetically attractive to the people you lead—and achieve more than you ever thought you could.

—Marshall Goldsmith, executive coach, business educator and New York Times-bestselling author, ranked the number one leadership thinker in the world by Thinkers50

Half a millennium ago William Gilbert discovered magnetism. That was helpful for inanimate objects, but pales in comparison to Roberta Matuson's application to our greatest asset: people.

The Magnetic Leader fulfills its promise with so much pragmatic advice that you can't separate it from your hands.

This book will attract those leaders who see people as assets and repel those who see them as expenses.

—Alan Weiss, PhD, author, *Million Dollar Consulting, Million Dollar Maverick*, and over 60 other books

There are two types of businesses. One values human talent above all else and is invariably successful. The other views people as a fungible commodity and the results are predictable—a miserable work environment and ultimate failure. If you're a leader (or follower) of an organization where you want to attract, retain, and leverage the best people, Roberta has insight and advice that you can use. Today.

—Mike Sheehan, CEO, Boston Globe

Roberta's book is refreshing in weaving together the stories of leaders who work to inspire, rather than direct employees. The book builds on the idea that lasting leadership starts with employee and customer engagement. Leaders must know to build and grow relationships and the notion of the magnetic leader builds around this theme. I recommend this book to anyone seeking to grow their circle of influence.

—Latha Ramchand, Dean and Professor, Finance; C.T. Bauer College of Business, University of Houston

Once again, Roberta Matuson challenges us to think differently about what it takes to create a winning organization. Her candid, common sense approach provides a great lens for us to use to evaluate any company and, most importantly, to assess our own effectiveness.

Roberta reminds us that individuals create culture, and focuses us on specific actions that can be taken to attract and retain the best possible team.

—Jerel Golub, Executive Vice Chairman of the Board at Price Chopper Supermarkets—Market 32

The Magnetic Leader is a timely book and a must read for every people leader. An organization is only as good as its people and its people can only reach their highest potential with equipped Magnetic Leaders. Its practical and easy to implement actions show how to put the "the human" back into talent management—giving you the "how to" for creating an environment that talent can thrive and wants to stay in.
— Yorlene Goff, Global Head of Talent Strategy and
Management, Havas Media

The heart of this book hits you within the second chapter. It outlines the challenges leaders face to engage, ignite and motivate employees! Like in any key relationship; customers, partners or personnel, you give more than you take as a leader.
— Matt Androski CEO of SMS, Sales Method Specialist

As a leader, there are countless opportunities to flail, but the author offers a comprehensive guide of tested, thoughtful strategies we can use to operate at a higher leader level. My favorite are the "Five Questions to Keep you on Track" in staying truly connected. I keep them handy and refer them as I prep for my day. Asking myself "Would I want my son working for someone like me?" keeps it very real!
— Sandy Rezendes, Head of Learning and Education,
Citizens Bank

Roberta understands the importance of engaged and happy employees and how they can elevate an organization's success, profile and reputation. In *The Magnetic Leader,* she shares even more insights on how leaders can attract, retain and most importantly improve the overall wellbeing of their employees.
— Paul F. Kraemer, Vice President, National Workplace
Voluntary Benefits Distribution Leader, Humana

A must read for current leaders who care about developing and retaining a 21st century workforce. *The Magnetic Leader* provides essential and practical wisdom for creating more productive and happy workers.
— Betsy Myers, Founding Director, Center for Women and
Business, Bentley University; Former Senior Advisor to
President Clinton and President Obama

The book is marvelous and Roberta is spot on. The impact that engagement and culture has not only on attracting but retaining our talent is an understatement. All leaders must get this about our 21st century workforce. The book is filled with engaging commentaries, and useful information on how to create this.
— Kip Hollister, Founder and CEO, Hollister Staffing

The Magnetic Leader

The Magnetic Leader

How Irresistible Leaders
Attract Employees,
Customers, and Profits

Roberta Chinsky Matuson

 bibliomotion
inc.

First edition published in 2017
by Bibliomotion, Inc.
711 Third Avenue New York, NY 10017, USA
2 Park Square, Milton Park, Abingdon, Oxon OX14 4RN, UK

© 2017 by Taylor & Francis Group, LLC

Bibliomotion is an imprint of Taylor & Francis Group, an Informa business

No claim to original U.S. Government works

Printed on acid-free paper

International Standard Book Number-13: 978-1-62956-165-3 (Hardback)
International Standard eBook Number-13: 978-1-3152-1280-7 (eBook)
International Standard Book Number-13: 978-1-62956-167-7 (Enhanced eBook)

Library of Congress Cataloging-in-Publication Data
Names: Matuson, Roberta Chinsky, author.
Title: The magnetic leader : how irresistible leaders attract employees, customers, and profits / Roberta Chinsky Matuson.
Description: New York : Bibliomotion, 2017. | Includes bibliographical references and index.
Identifiers: LCCN 2017004234 (print) | LCCN 2017006063 (ebook) | ISBN 9781629561653 (hardback) | ISBN 9781315212807 (ebook)
Subjects: LCSH: Leadership. | Employee motivation. | Success in business. | BISAC: BUSINESS & ECONOMICS / Leadership. | BUSINESS & ECONOMICS / Knowledge Capital. | BUSINESS & ECONOMICS / Management. | BUSINESS & ECONOMICS / Motivational.
Classification: LCC HD57.7 .M3934 2017 (print) | LCC HD57.7 (ebook) | DDC 658.4/092—dc23
LC record available at https://lccn.loc.gov/2017004234

Visit the Taylor & Francis Web site at
http://www.taylorandfrancis.com

Printed and bound by CPI Group (UK) Ltd, Croydon, CR0 4YY

This book is dedicated to my husband, Ron, who was a magnetic leader before being magnetic was cool, and to my children, Alexis and Zach, who inspire me every day with their magnetism and their zest for life. And to my parents, Sy and Jeanette Chinsky, who pushed me to think big.

Contents

Acknowledgments

I'd like to thank Erika Heilman of Bibliomotion, who said yes when I brought this book idea to her, and the team at Taylor and Francis, who took this book to completion. I'd also like to thank my editor, Susan Lauzau, who invested a ton of energy to make this book sparkle.

My deepest gratitude goes to my mentor, Alan Weiss, who told me for years that I wasn't an author until I published three books. Thanks to him, *today* I am an author. A big shout-out goes to my colleague and fellow author Noah Fleming, whose sense of humor and constant encouragement enabled me to complete this manuscript on time, and my colleague Hugh Blane, who was with me every step of the way.

I'd also like to thank all the magnetic leaders who so generously shared their stories. I hope they inspire you to be the best at what you do as much as they've inspired me.

About the Author

Roberta Chinsky Matuson, president of Matuson Consulting, has helped leaders in Fortune 500 companies, including General Motors, New Balance, The Boston Beer Company, and small to medium-sized businesses achieve dramatic growth and market leadership through the maximization of talent. She is known globally as "The Talent Maximizer®."

Roberta is an executive advisor who has personal experience in the C-suite. At only 24 years old, she was promoted to Director of Human Resources for a commercial real estate company, which she helped take public. She is known for her boldness and her ability to take on tough challenges that most people shy away from.

Roberta is the person that top employment site Monster and global retail giant Staples turn to for advice on talent. She is the author of *Suddenly In Charge: Managing Up, Managing Down, Succeeding All Around* (Nicholas Brealey, 2011), which was a Washington Post Top 5 Business Book For Leaders, and Talent Magnetism (Nicholas Brealey, 2013). She is also an expert blogger for *Forbes* and Glass Door, and is a former monthly columnist for *The Boston Business Journal*.

Introduction

Employees don't work for companies. They work for people. Yet companies keep piling on perks, hoping to buy their way into the hearts and minds of employees, and onto the infamous "best places to work" lists that resemble beauty contests more than they do reality. This strategy seems to have worked for many high-tech companies, which have managed to take employee incentives to a whole new level, but at what cost and for how long?

There's always a bigger boat or a better perk that can be had. However, there appears to be a vast shortage of great leaders. In a recent TinyPulse New Year Employee Report, one thousand working Americans shared their workplace wishes for the New Year.[1] Participants were asked what one thing they wished they could change about their manager. *The second most popular answer was to have their manager quit.* This response aligns with what I see in my consulting practice. Many enthusiastic employees are working for managers who are unclear about how to connect with their people in a way that is memorable for the right reasons.

I've spent the past nineteen years helping organizations achieve dramatic growth and market leadership by maximizing their talent. My clients span all industries and include companies like General Motors, Boston Beer Company, and Microsoft, as well as lesser-known organizations (at least for now) that are looking to dramatically improve the customer experience and boost their revenues. They all have one thing in common. They wish to achieve the desired state of magnetism—where the pull is so strong that top workers and customers can't help but find them irresistible. Companies like Apple, Google, and SAS are already there. However, contrary to popular belief, these companies didn't become magnetic overnight, nor did they get there without magnetic leaders. You're already on the right path. You are investing your time in reading this book. Should you desire a more multidimensional experience, contact me at Roberta@matusonconsulting.com to discuss the many ways we can work together.

Becoming a thought leader in the area of talent magnetism wasn't something I set out to do. It happened by circumstance. At the ripe old age of twenty-four, I was catapulted into the deep end of the pool (also known as the executive suite), and took a job I was completely unprepared for—director of human resources. After treading water for six years, I eventually learned to swim. I can tell you, based on my own experience of having been put suddenly in charge and being tossed into management with little more than a prayer, that the majority of leaders don't enter leadership roles thinking of ways to repel talent and make their employees miserable—after all, miserable employees will, in turn, make customers unhappy. That was certainly never my intention. However, I'm sure I left a number of unhappy people in my wake. This weighed heavily on me for years, and when my first book, *Suddenly in Charge*, was published, I wrote a post for BNET titled, "An Apology from a First-Time Boss." I must have struck a chord, as a ton of readers posted comments saying they wished their boss would apologize. And then it happened. After reading the post, one of my former employees reached out to me and said, "You really weren't *that* bad." Need I say more?

Over the years, I've thought about how I could make amends for my actions. Then one day it hit me. I could make a significant difference in the world of work by making the workplace more human. For this to happen, a dramatic shift would have to take place. Leaders would have to take valiant measures and break the tablet of rules handed down to them from the ivory towers of their organizations and instead use common sense. Their commitment to being the type of leader others want to work for would transform workplaces around the globe. They would need someone in the background, cheering them on to victory. That person would be me.

Throughout my career, I've helped hundreds of managers and executives transform themselves into magnetic leaders. I don't know who is more grateful, the leaders I've worked with or their people! The transformation for many has been life changing. So much so that I've been given the name *The Talent Maximizer®*. I'm thrilled to share my thoughts with you in this book about what it takes to make this transformation, so that you will have the opportunity to become a magnetic leader, and I can continue my promise of making the world of work a better place, one leader at a time.

I'm often asked, "Can magnetic leadership be taught?" Absolutely! Throughout this book, I will be by your side, guiding you as you make the journey from manager to magnetic leader. I'll be sharing some of the intimate details of mistakes I've made along the way, in the hope that your journey will be much smoother than mine. Included are stories from those who have made this transition, as well as some who are still on the journey. Should you happen to hit a few bumps in the road (and you will), know that you can learn just as much about magnetic leadership from your mistakes as you can from your successes—that is, if you are open to reflecting when things don't go according to plan and thinking about what you can do better the next time around.

No conversation about leadership would be complete without a discussion of corporate culture, a topic we'll explore in more detail throughout this book. I like to use the definition of *culture* promoted by my mentor, Dr. Alan Weiss, who talks about culture as a set of beliefs that govern behavior. The beliefs ingrained in the organization are based on the values and actions of the leaders who are in charge. Corporate culture flows through the veins of the organization and impacts everyone and everything, especially the customer experience, which in turn impacts profits.

In many companies, culture is created by default. Leaders are added to the mix with little thought about how they will impact culture. This is a huge mistake, and one that can and should be avoided. The most successful companies understand the impact leaders have on company culture. They are also aware of the direct connection that company culture plays in attracting employees, customers, and profits. That explains why they are willing to make the investment required to create workplaces that attract and keep the best.

It's important to note that organizations have subcultures, which is why it's not uncommon to hear one person say that a particular organization has a great company culture while someone else is telling a friend how awful it is to work for the very same company. Subcultures vary, depending on who is in charge of a particular department or working group. With this in mind, the first rule of thumb is to be careful whom you let in the door, especially when it comes to hiring managers. One bad leader can have a dramatic negative impact on the entire culture. Remember this as we discuss what it takes to create and sustain magnetic leaders, who are the common thread in organizations where employees love to work and customers love to do business. Let's get started.

Note

1. TinyPulse, "New Year Employee Report," 2015, https://www.tinypulse.com/landing-page/2015-new-year-employee-report.

Part 1
Magnetic Leadership

Chapter 1
The Magnetic Leader

I've asked dozens of people to tell me what comes to mind when they hear the words "magnetic leader," and no two responses have been exactly the same. Some people say, "I'll know one when I see one," which isn't all that helpful, considering we can't get into the minds of those responding! Here's my definition: a magnetic leader is someone whose leadership style is irresistible. You can't help but be attracted to this person and want to be on her team.

As I'm writing this, I happen to be flying over the Grand Canyon. As I look out of the plane window, I'm reminded of the huge chasms one finds in the leadership of organizations. There are leaders who are deep thinkers and who encourage others to look out over the horizon and enjoy the journey, while others simply blaze their own trail and expect that employees will fall in line. The first kind of leaders have given careful consideration to what it means to be responsible for the success or failure of those they lead. They charge ahead every day with the intent of helping their people chart their own course to personal and business success. They seek to work with like-minded people, and, as a management team, they demonstrate high levels of leadership in everything they do.

To help us fully comprehend what it takes to achieve magnetic leadership status, let's deconstruct the makeup of these different types of leaders. As we do this, you will gain a better sense of what it takes to achieve similar levels of success and can adjust your behaviors accordingly.

Traits of the Magnetic Leader

Lots of leaders think they are magnetic, when in fact they are anything but. Here are seven traits that are common among magnetic leaders, as well as examples of people who personify (or personified) these qualities. I'm sure you can think of a dozen more traits that would fit into this category. In chapter 5, we'll go into more detail regarding the way these characteristics impact "stickiness." I'll also suggest ways to acquire or fine-tune your magnetism. I encourage you to explore all of these methods and to focus on the two or three attributes that are the most meaningful to you.

1. **Authenticity.** Magnetic leaders don't try to be someone else, nor do they change who they are based on office politics. They are true to themselves and are honest in their dealings with others. They are not afraid to share their mistakes or shortcomings. Warren Buffet is an authentic leader who speaks openly about his $200 billion mistake buying Berkshire Hathaway.

2. **Selflessness.** Nelson Mandela immediately comes to mind when I think about inspirational leaders who are selfless. Leadership is a service business, and service comes with sacrifice. Mandela made many sacrifices so that others could advance, including giving up power. When elected president of South Africa, he refused to serve more than one term because he believed that a swift transfer of his authority was in the best interest of post-apartheid South Africa.

3. **Strong communication.** Magnetic leaders communicate frequently and clearly. They speak their minds, even if it makes them unpopular. When they are forthright with their opinions, such people often become even more magnetic. Pope Francis is a great example of an outspoken leader with strong communication skills, and his popularity has risen tenfold, as have donations to the church. People around the world are embracing Pope Francis. He doesn't toe the party line. He says what's on his mind, which is refreshing.

4. **Charisma.** They have a charm that inspires devotion. No matter where people fall on the political spectrum, most would agree that former President Bill Clinton possesses great charisma.

5. **Transparency.** Leaders who are transparent are *consistently* honest and open in their communication—so much so that people never have to guess what these leaders really mean when they say something. This level of openness often spreads to the wider company culture. Tony Hsieh, CEO of Zappos, is the first person who comes to mind when I think of transparent leaders. From the very beginning, before blogs became all the rage, Hsieh would openly share the

happenings (both the good and the bad) at Zappos for both employees and customers to see. In fact, the company's all-staff meetings were broadcast on the Internet.

6. **Vision.** Vision and magnetism go hand in hand. Visionary leaders, like the late Steve Jobs, are the dreamers who make us realize that anything is possible. They have a vivid imagination that inspires others to get on board and come along for the ride.

7. **Resilience.** Magnetic leaders understand that there will be times when things won't go according to plan. You simply must keep charging ahead, often course-correcting as you go. No one knows this better than GM chair and CEO Mary Barra, who had an incredibly stressful first year in office. She faced revelations about faulty ignition switches, a 30-million-car recall, and pressure from investors to return more cash to shareholders. But two years into her tenure, GM's financial health has rarely been stronger.

As you can see from this list, magnetism isn't something you are either born with or not. It's a state of leadership that evolves over time. The key word here is *evolves,* as most of the magnetic leaders I've interviewed for this book were like many of you when they first started out. They wanted to be good leaders and were willing to put in the work needed to reach that goal. They observed other leaders. Some, they emulated; others, they promised they would not be like. They learned by doing and made course corrections along the way. Many were fortunate enough to have a mentor who gave them honest feedback. Others hired coaches at different times in their careers. All of these leaders invested in their own development, and they continue to work on improving themselves every day. They do so because they understand the power of magnetism and how it can be a game changer when it comes to attracting employees, customers, and profits.

A common theme among the magnetic leaders I interviewed for this book is their willingness to be open about their failures. For example, Rob Nixon, CEO of PANALITIX, a membership community for accountants, told me that his inspiration to change his leadership style and the culture of the organization came from his worst "people" year, which took place in 2010. "I had twenty-six people movements in a team of sixteen," Nixon said. "Not good." This jolt led him to consider the type of organization he wanted to create. He wrote down the type of culture he wanted for his business, basing the culture on the values and standards important to him. He then posted the blueprint for his company culture on his website so that employees and customers could see what his firm stands for. Nixon is glad his worst "people" years are behind him, although, like any good leader, he'll admit that he is a work in progress.

The Power of Magnetic Leadership

If you are going to put in the work to become a magnetic leader, then you probably want to know up front what kind of ROI you can expect. After reading this section, you will no doubt agree that the return on magnetism (ROM) is significant and well worth the investment.

Better Hires, Faster

Retired Biogen CIO Raymond Pawlicki was able to quickly differentiate himself from other CIOs through magnetism. Over the years, Pawlicki worked really hard to build a following. He made it a point to spend a good deal of his time out of the office. He made a name for himself and the company he worked for. He did so by volunteering to speak at conferences, visiting college campuses, and meeting with anyone who asked him for a few minutes of his time. Whenever Pawlicki had a job opening in his department (and it was rare), he had a line of people waiting outside his door hoping he'd hire them. He shared with me that he had rarely paid a recruitment fee to an employment agency during his long career—something most of his peers could not say.

A year after Pawlicki's retirement, I met several of his former employees, who were still lamenting the fact that they were no longer working for him. I told them to get over it. Pawlicki wasn't coming back. Instead of complaining, they could honor him by giving their employees a work experience similar to the one Pawlicki had given them. One guy took out his phone and made notes so he could remember to purchase the leadership books I recommended. He understood that the torch had been passed and that it was his turn to become a magnetic leader.

Magnetic leaders like Pawlicki have no problem attracting talent. I'm betting you know at least a handful of people like him. The cost of hiring people is minimal for these leaders. All it takes is one tweet or a call to a few employees they may have worked with in the past, and resumes start flying into their inboxes. If you think about it, most third-party recruiters charge between 25 and 30 percent of an employee's first year's salary plus bonuses. Recruitment fees add up quite rapidly. Think about how much additional money will hit your bottom line annually when you are able to avoid going this costly route—not to mention the decrease in stress you will feel, knowing that you aren't going to be involved in a bidding war for talent.

Off-the-Chart Employee Commitment and Staff Productivity

I was fortunate to have the opportunity to work for a magnetic leader. This leader had my full commitment, and the commitment of everyone else in the organization, in spite of the fact that we were paid significantly less than market rate. You may be thinking, "Why on earth would you give someone your all, knowing that you could make a heck of a lot more money elsewhere?" But knowing what I know today, I'd do the same thing all over again.

This leader made it clear that we were on a mission to change our industry. He listened to our ideas and treated us with respect. We worked long hours and never minded doing so. I had friends who were making tons of money working for big-name companies, but they were miserable. I looked at them every day and knew that my life was much richer than theirs, even if they had more money in the bank than I did. We were completely committed to this leader and the organization.

Reduction in Costly Employee Turnover

According to the *State of the American Manager* report by Gallup, approximately half of all workers have left a job to "get away from a manager."[1] My bet is that none of these people were leaving a magnetic leader. Those who have run away from a bad boss will stick like glue to any great leader they find after experiencing what it's like to work for a boss who actually repels talent.

Increased Innovation

When you are working for someone who thinks bigger than most, you often find yourself thinking bigger as well. This person encourages you to take risks. He makes it okay to fail.

Inspiration is a key part of innovation as well. Imagine for a moment what it must be like to work for Elon Musk, cofounder of PayPal and founder of the electric car company Tesla and the space technology company SpaceX. He and his team keep coming up with ideas that are out of this world!

High Levels of Customer Satisfaction

Magnetic leaders put customers first and encourage their people to do the same. I'm a frequent patron of Barcelona Restaurant and Wine Bar, which currently has twelve locations. It's a very busy restaurant and, as at most eating establishments, things occasionally go wrong. When my experience at the restaurant doesn't go smoothly, I never think to myself, "I can't wait to go on Yelp and tell the world about my negative experience." That's because I know that the manager or one of the wait staff will do the right thing. They'll take the disappointing item off the bill without being asked to do so, or they'll bring a replacement dish or an additional unexpected treat. They don't really have to go the extra mile, as there are plenty of customers waiting for tables. Or perhaps this is *exactly* the reason that people are willing to wait ninety minutes for an opportunity to dine at the restaurant.

More Repeat Business and Referrals

I like to do business with companies that have employees who seem happy to work with me. Happy employees are rarely found in places where dreadful leaders rule the roost. Whenever I've encountered a miserable manager or employee, I've quickly taken my business elsewhere. When I do find a place with great management, I tend to go back, even if less expensive options are available to me. And, of course, I let all my friends know they should do business there as well.

Market Leadership

It's not easy to be in business these days. There are competitors all around waiting to knock you off your perch. Market leadership status is something that must be earned. Apple is a prime example of a company that has earned its place as a market leader in the tech industry. If you've ever visited an Apple Store, you know why. Managers are on the floor, right next to sales staff, and are ready to step in and serve you. Compare this practice with that of retailers that post managers upstairs in a booth, watching from above as customers circle like sharks waiting to attack their prey — also known as the all-too-scarce clerks on the retail floor.

Magnetic leadership and market leadership are like the chicken and the egg: it's hard to know which comes first, as organizations become market leaders based on their magnetic leadership, and magnetic leaders find themselves being pulled toward companies that are market leaders. In either case, magnetism is necessary.

Corporate Growth

Magnetic leadership isn't just a feel-good thing. Leadership helps shape culture, and culture in turn shapes leadership. Both drive performance, including revenues and profitability. A recent study by Egon Zehender International and McKinsey & Company titled *Return on Leadership — Competencies that Generate Growth*[2] confirms that talent matters, especially when it comes to leadership. According to the study, executives of high-growth companies have a higher level of competency than those of low-performing firms. The study also revealed that having good leaders is not enough; only excellence makes the difference. Outstanding leadership teams are highly correlated with revenue growth, while solid but unexceptional leadership is not correlated with growth at all. It's also interesting to note that the myth that a small group of high-potential executives — or just a star CEO — can drive business success is just that, a myth. According to the study, a critical *mass* of excellent leaders is needed to trigger and sustain corporate growth.

Creating a Force of Magnetic Leaders

It's easy to become overwhelmed when thinking about hiring a force of magnetic leaders, since you may currently have only one or two on your team. Here's what it takes to hire excellent leaders:

Clarity. "I'll know it when I see it" doesn't really fly. You have to have agreement up front among the executive team about the traits you are seeking in your leaders, so you can hire accordingly.

Speed. Speed, not money, is the biggest differentiator when it comes to hiring talented leaders. Companies and their hiring managers are taking *way* too long to fill jobs. As a result, their first choice is often no longer available if and when they finally get around to extending an offer.

Patience. You may think it's a bit odd that I'm writing about patience after telling you that it's necessary to move with lightning speed to fill jobs. Here's why you need patience as you assemble a force of magnetic leaders.

It's easy to get discouraged when trying to hire talented leaders, particularly in a hot job market where good candidates appear to be as rare as a sixty-degree day in the middle of a New England winter. However, if you are not patient and you end up hiring the wrong person for your management team, you will lose more than just that person when you wind up firing him. You'll have disgruntled employees who will not be serving your clients or customers in a way that makes you proud. You will also find yourself right back where you started, trying to fill a leadership role in a hot job market. Do yourself and everyone else a favor. Be patient and wait for the right candidate.

Assessing Your Current Leaders

I'm often brought into organizations to boost the effectiveness of their leadership teams. Rarely do I find myself in a position where I think every leader is a keeper. That's not to say these people weren't good leaders when they first came to the firm. Some were particularly strong in start-up mode, but the company is now in maintenance mode; others were suitable leaders when the firm was in cost-cutting mode, but aren't so effective in growth mode. Whatever the reason, you most likely have people on your team who are no longer magnetic. Here are some questions you should be asking yourself on a regular basis:

- Would I hire this person today?
- Will this person help us get to the next level?
- If someone better came along and I didn't have to go through HR or legal, would I make a trade?
- Has this person gone as far as he is going, and would I be doing him a favor if I released him back into the universe?

Magnetic Leadership

It's good to know where things stand, so you can focus on the areas that matter most. Here's a tool that I've developed to help my clients assess the status of their leaders. How does your organization fare when it comes to magnetic leadership?

ORGANIZATIONAL MAGNETIC LEADERSHIP SELF-ASSESSMENT Please rate your company in each of the following areas:	Ratings 4 = All the time 3 = Most of the time 2 = Sometimes 1 = Rarely 0 = Never N/A = Not applicable
We know who our top leaders are.	
We support the growth of our top leaders.	
We treat our leaders as "assets" in which we need to invest rather than as "costs" that can be easily reduced.	
We know the *real* reason employees are leaving our company, and we use this information to make improvements wherever possible.	
We take immediate action when a leader has more turnover than most.	
Our leaders receive *continuous* feedback on their performance.	
Employees feel great about their leader.	
The people we promote are magnetic leaders.	

(Continued)

ORGANIZATIONAL MAGNETIC LEADERSHIP SELF-ASSESSMENT *Please rate your company in each of the following areas:*	Ratings 4 = All the time 3 = Most of the time 2 = Sometimes 1 = Rarely 0 = Never N/A = Not applicable
We regularly ask our employees what we can do to improve our workplace.	
Our executives view employee magnetism as a top priority.	
The people we'd like to retain rarely leave our company.	
We quickly transition leaders who don't make the grade out of the organization.	
Our customers/clients rave about our employees.	
We are viewed as an exceptional place to work.	
We don't have to go after top talent because they usually approach us.	
Employees understand how their work contributes to the bottom line of the company.	
Employees would rate their managers as being great to work for.	
Our managers are trained to select, identify, guide, coach, reward, and retain their people.	
We provide coaches to our top leaders.	
Employees have the tools and skills to perform their jobs satisfactorily.	
My organization knows how much it costs to replace every employee who leaves the organization.	
I believe this is a great place to work.	

Any area with a score of 2 or less requires immediate attention!

What You Need to Know When Promoting Leaders

I've seen people promoted into management for a variety of reasons, many of which do not make sense. For example, company management sometimes assumes that a top salesperson will automatically be a top leader of the sales department. Rarely is this the case, and the organization may wind up losing a great salesperson as well as many of the people who work for that new leader. Of course there are also the promotions given because no one really wanted the job or because someone was promised a promotion when she was hired, only the person really isn't management material. But, hey, a promise is a promise! Here are five things to consider before you promote someone into a leadership position:

1. **Desire.** I'm putting desire first, because if someone doesn't really want a leadership role, the rest of the list doesn't matter. Magnetic leadership requires authenticity. You simply cannot fake enjoying being in a leadership role. You have to really want the job.

2. **Aptitude.** The capacity and readiness to lead others must not be overlooked when promoting people into leadership roles, yet too often it is. Younger people get passed over for leadership roles because of preconceived notions that age is correlated with maturity and management readiness, while older workers are promoted without thoughtful consideration as to whether they have the aptitude for the job. Think about this before you promote your next employee.

3. **Traits.** The traits (competencies) necessary to be successful in a leadership role vary, depending upon the level of the position and the industry. Take a look at your most successful leaders. What traits do they have in common? Does the person you are considering for promotion have similar traits? If not, will this person be the right fit for a management role in your company?

4. **Attitude.** Management is not for the weary. It's not easy coming to work every day with a smile on your face and a can-do attitude when you may be overworked or business is trending downward. Yet this is exactly what a good leader must do. Does the person you are about to promote have a positive attitude about life in general? If not, select someone else for the job.

5. **Stamina.** Not everyone has the stamina to be a leader. You have to be prepared to step in and do the job of others, should they move on to greener pastures. You must be able to multitask and switch gears at a moment's notice. Low-energy people need not apply.

Now that you have a better understanding of what it means to be a magnetic leader and the ROM you can expect when you achieve magnetic status, we'll move on and discuss how magnetic leadership impacts employees, customers, and profits.

> ### Gravitational Pull Exercise #1
>
> Complete the Organizational Magnetic Leadership Self-Assessment. Take note of the areas in which you scored a 2 or below and develop a plan to address these issues immediately.

Notes

1. Gallup, "State of the American Manager: Analytics and Advice for Leaders," April 2015, http://www.gallup.com/services/182138/state-american-manager.aspx.
2. Egon Zehender International and McKinsey & Company, "Return on Leadership—Competencies that Generate Growth," February, 10, 2011, https://www.mckinsey.de/sites/mck_files/files/Return%20on%20Leadership.pdf.

Chapter 2

The Magnetic Connection Principle: You and Your People, Customers, and Profits

You can tell a lot about an organization's leadership and its bottom line without even reading the financials. Here's what I mean by this: I remember visiting a prospect's office and walking away wondering how this start-up was still in business. I make it a point to arrive early when I meet with prospects so I have time to look around and observe what's going on. I've been doing this for years, and nothing could have prepared me for what I experienced on this particular occasion. I saw an ocean of cubicles filled with young professionals, yet there was no laughter, nor was there much going on in the way of conversation. En route to the CEO's office I walked past the company kitchen, where the only sound I could hear was that of the microwave, despite the fact that there were at least half a dozen employees in the room. The silence was alarming.

After meeting with the CEO, I understood that this organization was not very healthy, from either a cultural or a financial perspective. He came across as being aloof and not particularly concerned that many of his employees were departing. I couldn't get out of there fast enough, and seriously thought of rescuing a few employees on my way out. I recently looked at the company's profile on Glassdoor, a website where employees can post about their work experiences. My suspicions were right: the last several years at this company have apparently been nothing but turmoil, a direct result of employee churn and, most probably, poor leadership.

Gallup, known for its groundbreaking research in the area of employee engagement, has conducted studies that show a direct correlation between employee engagement, profits, and a host of other critical business outcomes. Gallup defines engaged employees as those who are involved in, enthusiastic about, and committed to their work and workplace. According to Gallup, powerful links exist between engaged employees and achievement of key business outcomes. Companies with highly engaged workforces outperform their peers by 147 percent in earnings per share and realize

- 41% fewer quality defects
- 28% less shrinkage
- 65% less turnover (low-turnover organizations)
- 25% less turnover (high-turnover organizations)
- 37% less absenteeism

When employees are engaged, they are passionate, innovative, and entrepreneurial, and their eagerness fuels growth. These employees are emotionally connected to the purpose of their work. When employees are not engaged, they are apathetic toward their jobs—or, worse, they outright hate their work, manager, and organization, and some of these employees can and will stop at nothing to destroy a work unit and a business.

Henry Kallan, president of the Library Hotel Collection, has a deep understanding of the connection between employees, customers, and profits. Kallan, who built his company from the ground up, says, "If I'm to expect my employees to take care of my clients, it's only appropriate that I take care of my employees." Kallan also understands that you can't fake authenticity. He reminds his employees that you can never fool anyone. "People will know whether you have good intentions or that you don't," Kallan says. You also can't fake happiness, which means that if you are disenchanted with your work environment, you'll be hard pressed to create the type of customer experience that will keep people coming back. Kallan prides himself on the fact that 60 to 79 percent of his hotels' clients are repeat business. Recently, I tried to be a repeat customer at the New York City Hotel Giraffe, a member of the Library Hotel Collection. Unfortunately for me, no rooms were available.

Kallan believes that 80 percent of those in management ranks, once they achieve a certain position in life, feel entitled to enjoy their status to the fullest, so they put themselves before the needs of the business, the first of which is making sure employees are happy and that they feel they are part of the team. Do you believe that managers are putting their needs ahead of the needs of the business, and if so, how is this playing out in your organization?

Think about your experiences as a consumer, both good and bad, and how you felt about continuing to do business with a company after having an interaction with one of its employees. Did you have one or more encounters that led you to believe the employee clearly enjoyed his job and went above and beyond the call of duty on your behalf? If the answer is yes, I'm guessing you made it a point to continue to do business with that company and that you are making sure your friends do so as well. If the answer is no, you may have chosen to keep doing business with the company. However, it's highly unlikely that you go out of your way to recommend others do so as well. If the encounter was memorable for the wrong reasons, you've most likely taken your business elsewhere and made sure you warned others, through social media, to do the same. Remember this the next time you question whether you should care if your employees are happy.

Why Money Can't Buy Love— or Employee Happiness

I know a lot of miserable employees who stay with their employers only for the money. I can understand why this is so, as money can be very addicting. But what happens when these miserable employees reach the point where they feel like caged animals? They begin to lash out at one another and, worse, at your customers.

In this highly competitive talent market, it's easy to keep throwing more money at people in order to get them to stay. Tempting as it is, this approach is a huge mistake. There is always someone with a bigger wallet out there, which means it's only a matter of time before your salaries soar out of control. But more importantly, think about what it would be like for people to stay with you because they want to and not because they are unable to go elsewhere and earn similar pay.

I've worked for some leaders who were simply irresistible. I could have made a heck of a lot more money working elsewhere; however, I never really gave that much thought, as I learned early on that money cannot buy employee happiness. I'll admit there were times when I had to say no to a weekend getaway due to finances. But unlike some of my very well-compensated friends, I never had to talk myself into working every day at a job that I hated because the money was too good to leave.

The concept of buying your way into the hearts of employees is foreign to nonprofit leaders like Catherine D'Amato, CEO of the Greater Boston Food Bank, whose mission is to end hunger in Eastern Massachusetts. D'Amato is unable to simply open her checkbook in order to retain people. When it comes to employee retention and happiness, there is much to be learned from nonprofit leaders. "People like to be around successful people," notes D'Amato. They also want to work for people who have the reputation, like D'Amato, of bringing their people along on a life-changing journey.

I've had the pleasure of working as a strategic advisor to D'Amato, and have observed firsthand the way she connects with her team members. When she speaks with her staff, you get the sense that she is completely present. She listens intently and provides her people with the space they need to make their own decisions. She does this even when these decisions may not be the ones D'Amato would make. She readily admits that it's not always easy to give up control. "I lead with the belief that there are many roads to the same place," D'Amato says. People come to work for the Greater Boston Food Bank and D'Amato because they want to be part of this magnetic environment she has created. I did so for this very same reason.

The WOW Factor

As part of my work helping clients build workplaces where employees love to work and customers love to do business, I make it a point to speak directly to employees so I can learn how *they* experience work. It's their stories that create what I call the WOW (Word of Wonderfulness) Factor, which directly impacts the customer experience. Employees who have great words to say about their employers are brand ambassadors for their organizations. Here's what I mean.

No one knows more about the impact of employees on the customer experience and company reputation than Shannon Eis, VP of corporate communications at Yelp. Eis tells the story of planning her maternity leave, when she was a senior VP of communications for a small agency:

> I was the first employee to have a baby there, and at the time the firm didn't have a maternity leave policy. The CEO sat me down and said that she knew what she needed when she had her child fifteen years prior, but that didn't mean that she knew what I needed. Together, we designed the maternity leave. I was also asked for my input regarding how we should best manage the customer relationships on the agency side while I was on leave. We didn't miss a beat.

As a result of this experience, Eis always thinks about what she needs to do to put her employees first. She knows that by doing so, both the team and customers will thrive.

Founder and CEO of Broughton Hotels Larry Broughton understands the importance of treating his team members the way he'd like his guests to be treated. "This is a relationship business," notes Broughton. "The way we treat our team members is how our team members treat our clients."

Broughton's leadership journey began when he was in the U.S. Army Special Forces. "There are only twelve guys on a team," states Broughton. "We had a strong, magnetic team. I try to apply what I learned there and always think about the things that created those cohesive relationships."

Broughton goes on to say, "We are a learning organization at Broughton Hotels and we are trying to be better today than we were last week." He believes leaders need to institutionalize their efforts to reward, recognize, and reinforce the behaviors they'd like their employees to continually display. "We have a program called the Dollar Star Program. We want to catch people doing something right. We give each team member two origami stars made from dollar bills. When a team member is awarded an origami star, he in turn must give an origami star to a teammate. We do this because we want to encourage them to catch their teammates doing something right." Broughton Hotels has more than seven hundred employees and runs based on the premise that if you want to do great things, you have to be a great person. Broughton makes a point of working on this attitude daily, as he understands that the way his employees feel about their experience at work, and in turn the way they treat their guests, starts with him.

The Dollar Star Program extends beyond the employees. "We do reverse tipping as well," notes Broughton. "When we see a client or a guest do something kind, we give one of these origami stars to them as well."

Every day, happy employees are WOWing customers and creating favorable experiences that attract other customers. This strategy is the key to business growth for many companies. Referrals and strong word of mouth help small businesses—which, according to the SBA,[1] make up 99.7 percent of U.S. businesses—compete with the giants, which have marketing budgets equal in size to the payroll of many of these small businesses.

Assessing Happiness in and with Your Business

Employees and customers hate surveys. Don't believe me? Why don't you send out a survey to see? No, please don't! Following is just one of the many examples of why you will be wasting your time if you insist on going down this route yet again.

A friend of mine is a senior manager for a well-known financial institution that sends out an annual employee engagement survey. Because she's a leader, her scores and compensation are directly tied to the number of surveys returned. Full participation is the name of the game, and she knows what it takes to make it happen. Every year she gathers the troops and explains that it's annual engagement survey time. Some eyes roll, which doesn't seem to bother her anymore, as she expects this reaction. She then tells the team that if everyone fills out the survey, she will take the team to lunch. They all comply. She shares with me that the same issues come up year after year in the annual employee engagement survey and very little changes in the organization—except perhaps the location where they dine.

Another survey story that comes to mind concerns one of my friends, who received a survey from the dealership where she had just purchased her car. The dealership folks had taken the liberty of completing the survey on her behalf and had given themselves top scores! She went from satisfied customer to angry customer with just one interaction.

Please, I beg of you. Stop surveying and start doing. I'll bet you a free coaching session that if I were to ask you to list the areas in your organization that need improvement, your list would nearly mirror the survey results you'd receive, if indeed you conducted another survey. You *already* know what to do. Why do you keep asking for feedback? Instead of investing more money in surveys, use these resources to address one or two areas that need improvement. Once you've made significant progress in those areas, address additional areas that need attention.

What to Do When the Problem Is You

In spite of my warnings, many of you will continue to do surveys. Therefore, I thought it best to cover an all-too-common situation: the feedback comes back, and the problem is you. Yep! That's right. All fingers are pointing to you. After all, the buck stops with the leader.

It's only natural to want to stomp up and down the halls trying to find the guy who had the nerve to say what everyone was thinking. Whatever you do, don't take action until you've had time to process the feedback you've been given. This is both a learning and a growth opportunity. You now have unfiltered (notice I didn't say unsolicited) feedback that you can use to improve the work environment of those you serve.

Thank your team for sharing their opinions and let them know that you are taking the feedback you received to heart. You may be tempted to make this announcement via e-mail, but if at all possible do it in person at an all-team meeting. This will give you an opportunity to demonstrate to your employees that you genuinely appreciate their feedback and to share the steps you will be taking to make improvements.

Avoiding Common Feedback Mistakes

Everybody is a critic these days, and access to social media makes it easier than ever to share our opinions. Sometimes it's hard to determine how best to proceed when you receive tough feedback. Here are some common mistakes leaders make when it comes to criticism, together with ideas for what you can do to avoid making similar mistakes.

Launching a Counterattack

Most of us know someone who has a response to every word we say. Don't be that guy. When receiving solicited feedback, resist the temptation to respond to everything that is said. Instead, pick one or two important points and ask for clarification, including specific examples.

Reacting to Unsolicited Feedback

I'm the first to admit that I want to fix things the minute I think they are broken, and this is a common mistake leaders make when it comes to feedback. Jumping into action just because one person has given you unsolicited feedback can lead you to make the wrong move. Often the person is giving you feedback for her own benefit rather than yours. Ignore unsolicited feedback if the criticism comes from one person. If you see a pattern emerging, find a coach or trusted advisor who can help you make improvements.

Soliciting Feedback Infrequently

What do you think would happen if you only got on the scale once a year? Most likely, you'd be quite surprised by the results—and not necessarily in a good way. I see a similar thing happen in organizations where leaders ask for feedback annually instead of more frequently. They, too, are shocked by the results. Of course, you are probably thinking, "Who the heck has time to ask for feedback on a daily or weekly basis?" You do. You don't need a formal survey to obtain feedback. You can simply invite one of your employees to join you for a cup of coffee and, while he is there, ask him how things are going. For those of you who have employees both near and far, you may want to take note of tools like TinyPulse, which lets you ping short questions weekly to your employees and gather feedback in more digestible bites, or Skype, a platform from which you can host brief check-in sessions.

Making the Simple Complicated

We seem to love to hear ourselves talk. At least, that's the explanation I come up with when I think about why we ask employees the same questions, and often the wrong questions, in ten different ways. Instead, determine exactly what you want to know, then ask the one or two questions that will provide you with the answers you are seeking. In most cases, asking, "On a scale of one to ten, with ten being high, how likely would you be to recommend this company as a place of work?" Follow that question with, "What would it take for you to respond with a ten?" and you will have all the information you need to assess employee happiness in your workplace. Of course, companies that make millions on survey instruments and associated services will try to convince you that it's much more complicated than it actually is. Ignore them.

Being Social

That old advice "If you can't beat them, join them" rings true these days. Everyone seems to be participating in one form of social media or another, and the question is no longer whether or not you should participate; it's when and how. Younger workers today think nothing of sharing their every opinion on social media. The question is, should you do the same? Well, it depends. Are you sharing the great things you are doing on behalf of your employees and customers or are you fighting what feels like an attack?

Before she took on the role of VP of corporate communications for Yahoo, Shannon Eis's media relations specialty was crisis management. She explained to me that the first rule of thumb in crisis management is to never fuel the flames. If you don't stoke the fire, eventually the blaze will die down on its own. This advice applies to leaders in their use of social media: the best defense for an employee who has taken her complaint to social media is to refrain from launching an online defense. If the matter needs handling, do so privately.

Young people today rely mainly on social media for their news. Many trust implicitly what they see, and that tendency makes social media an important vehicle for building relationships these days. You, as the leader of an organization, can use social media to your advantage, especially when it comes to recruiting talent. For example, posting pictures of your team working with you on an interesting project or volunteering in your community gives others a glimpse of what it might feel like to work for you. Keep in mind that not everyone is going to like what he sees. That's okay. These people wouldn't have been the right hires for you anyway, so be grateful they are not going to engage with you further. Think of all the time and money you just saved!

Here's another perspective on social media from Niki Leondakis, CEO of Commune Hotels, who, by the way, I first met via social media. Leondakis is one of those rare CEOs who monitors her Twitter feed personally and posts her own responses. "Guests as well as employees tweet me," says Leondakis. She also uses social media to engage her global workforce and to connect with customers. "I do Twitter chats every sixty days with my whole company. The chat goes for two hours and is open to the public." Leondakis goes on to say, "I think transparency is critical. The chat also seems to engage the public. They see the open dialogue between the CEO and the employees, which further enhances our brand."

It's important for those of you interested in increasing your magnetism to keep in mind that brand awareness is important these days. Leondakis is a great example of the importance of brand, and her practice shows how you can strengthen your brand without spending oodles of dollars to do so. This includes your personal brand. Here are some things to keep in mind as you look to enhance your magnetism through social channels.

Remember That Not All Social Channels Are Equal

You've probably noticed that commercials for pharmaceutical products are aired at particular times and during select television shows. That's because pharmaceutical companies know their target market and where these people are most likely hanging out. You need to apply these same principles to the piece of your magnetic leadership campaign that relates to social media. Determine the audience you are trying to connect with and make it a point to be present on the channels where they typically hang out. Ignore the other social media channels or if you choose, you can designate certain platforms for personal use only.

Be Consistent

Showing up on social media twice a year isn't going to do anything in terms of building a following. You have to be intentional. At a minimum, you should be posting three times a week. Make a note in your calendar until contributing on social media becomes habit.

Give More Than You Take

The quickest way to build a following and increase your personal brand is to give before asking others for help. Here's what I mean by this: Reposting another's tweet or offering to share a person's article with your followers on LinkedIn will eventually get you noticed. These same people will be the first to return the favor when you ask them to share news about an event or a job opening with their followers.

Be Bold

No doubt about it, there is a lot of noise on social media. The real way to get noticed is to be bold. Don't shy away from taking a stand, even if it's not the popular thing to do. And don't forget to be authentic, which in turn will help you to attract a following worth having.

Beyond Happiness

As you think about your own business and your leadership style, consider how your own personal happiness and that of your employees impact customer satisfaction and company profits; then ask yourself the following questions:

- Are you happy? If so, how does being happy impact your relationship with team members and customers? If not, what do you need to do to get happy? Be open to all possibilities, including finding another line of work.
- Are there people in your organization or on your team who will never be happy? Jot their names down and take steps to exit them from the organization. Begin this process today.
- What are you doing, specifically, that is creating a happier and more satisfied workforce? Take note of these things and do more of the same. Stop doing things that no longer make a difference.

Employees as Business Owners

Business leaders often tell me that they wish their people would act more like business owners rather than employees. When they say this to me, I ask them why they would expect someone who isn't an owner to behave as if she were. I then remind them that if this person wanted to be a business owner, she most likely wouldn't be working for the company. She'd have her own business!

Sometimes, you can have it both ways; you can be an employee *and* a business owner. Dan Kenary, cofounder and CEO of Harpoon Brewery, has found the secret to getting employees to act like business owners. Here's his story. In 2014, his cofounder was ready to exit the business. There were a number of ways Kenary could make this transaction happen, including selling to a much larger brewer or an equity firm. He quickly dismissed both these ideas and instead decided to give his workers an opportunity to change their lives forever.

Several of the Boston-based brewer's shareholders, including his cofounder, sold 48 percent of the company to an employee stock ownership plan (ESOP). All 187 of Harpoon's full-time employees were then *given* shares in the company. "I'm trying to give our employees a chance to fully participate in the value we create," states Kenary. "I saw this as an opportunity to give back to the community and give people a shot at something they may never have had. The impact we've had on people's lives is what matters to me."

That's what I call putting your money where your mouth is. Kenary told me, over a beer, that the easiest thing he could have done was to sell the company, take his money, and drive away into the sunset. Instead, he put the lives of others before his own interests, and he continues to do so every day as he teaches his employees the skills necessary to be business owners. I have no doubt that another group of entrepreneurs will flourish as a result of the opportunity Kenary is giving his people, and hopefully they will follow his path of selfless leadership. Think of how much better our world would be if we had more leaders like Kenary.

Employee satisfaction is the first step on the journey to magnetic leadership. As part of this voyage, you must look at what you are doing well so you can repeat these actions, and you must also look at those areas where you may not be performing as well as you had hoped.

I always tell my clients that it's our behavior that matters and not our intentions. In the next chapter, we'll explore what happens in organizations when leaders go off the rails in spite of their best intentions.

Gravitational Pull Exercise #2

Talk to your employees about how they experience work. Ask them what, specifically, you can do to create for them the type of WOW experience you are trying to create for your customers.

Note

1. SBA-97. In 2012, according to U.S. Census Bureau data, there were 5.73 million employer firms in the United States. Firms with fewer than 500 workers accounted for 99.7 percent of those businesses. SBE Council, http://sbecouncil. org/about-us/facts-and-data/.

Chapter 3
The Teflon Effect:
Nonstick Leadership

I've worked with and for a number of leaders whose leadership style was anything but magnetic. I call these nonstick leaders Teflon leaders. That's because they were experts at repelling talent. As mentioned in the introduction, I believe we can learn as much from poor leaders as we can from great leaders. And even though we may not place ourselves in the poor leadership category, we certainly may be guilty of displaying similar behavior from time to time.

Christie Smith, PhD and managing principal of multinational professional services firm Deloitte, calls things as she sees them. Her unfiltered approach to leadership is like a cool glass of lemonade on a hot summer's day. It's refreshing! Smith has worked with hundreds of companies and has found that arrogance runs rampant in organizations. "Most senior executives in major corporations and start-ups aren't in touch," notes Smith. "People only tell them what they think they want to hear. Therefore, they are completely out of touch." Smith goes on to say, "There is nothing more damaging to a brand than a leader who is fundamentally out of touch."

In my own practice, I've observed a similar phenomenon regarding out of touch leaders. It's the rare enlightened CEO who isn't afraid to raise her hand and ask for help, particularly when it comes to improving her effectiveness as a leader. When I coach these leaders, I'm not only helping the leader; I'm helping the employees who work for the person. Interestingly, as a result of my work with executives, their direct reports often raise their hands and ask for help as well.

Smith says her goal is to call out arrogant leaders. "Leaders do need a slap aside the head, as many are thinking, 'I've got five more years and I can leave with $70 million.'" Millennials, who have now become the largest generation in the American workforce,[1] crave authenticity and happiness. "Millennials are happy to wait tables rather than work in an organization that is not authentic," notes Smith.

A number of the executives I interviewed for this book told stories about leaders who are actively repelling talent. It's really shocking how frequently this occurs in organizations, especially given the fragile state of the talent market. For example, a friend of mine recently took a position with a big-name company and was thrilled to be working in such a great environment. That was before his boss called to slap him back in line because he'd had a conversation with a fellow employee who wasn't in his silo (his words, not mine). He's still showing up for work every day, but I predict that by the time this book is published he will have taken his talent elsewhere. All it takes is one call from a headhunter on a day when your employee has reached his limit and boom—he is gone.

Take a look at the leadership deficiencies that are causing employees to flee their bosses. Then ask yourself what you can do to ensure this doesn't happen to you.

Disengaged Leadership of Epidemic Proportions

According to the 2015 Gallup report *The State of the American Manager*, 65 percent of U.S. managers are disengaged in their jobs. This is simply shocking to me! Managers have the biggest impact on employee engagement, which makes this state particularly worrisome. And it raises the question, how does a company serve its employees and its customers when the people in charge have checked out? The answer is "not well," which is why workers are fleeing their bosses in droves. Another 2015 Gallup poll concluded that the number-one reason people quit their jobs is a bad boss or immediate supervisor. "People leave managers not companies . . . in the end, turnover is mostly a manager issue," Gallup wrote in its survey findings. The impact of poor management is widely felt. Gallup also determined that poorly managed work groups are on average 50 percent less productive and 44 percent less profitable than well-managed groups.

For a minute, let's suppose you are one of the disengaged leaders cited in the report. What can you do? The way I see it, you have two choices.

You can tell your manager why you feel the way you do and work with her to change things or you can resign. Staying and doing nothing is *not* an option, as there are too many people counting on you to lead by example.

Lack of Aptitude for the Job

Last week, I had yet another conversation with a client who described someone he'd put in a leadership role whom he never should have hired. Simply put, the guy didn't have the talent to do the job he was hired to do—lead a team of engineers. While I believe leadership skills can be acquired, I don't believe everyone is well suited for the role of leader. In fact, when you promote or hire into a leadership role a person who should never be placed in such a position, you usually wind up losing much more than the leader you now have to fire. You lose the great employee he used to be as well as the people who departed the moment they realized they were unable to work for this person. You also lose customers who no longer feel supported by your organization. Lucky for my client, he was able to convince a few of the people who'd left to return. All he had to do was tell them their former boss was no longer with the organization!

According to the 2015 Gallup State of the American Manager report, only about 10 percent of managers showed indicators that they could motivate every individual on their team, boldly review performance, build relationships, overcome adversity, and make decisions based on productivity. Gallup CEO Jim Clifton said in the report, "A manager with little talent for the job will deal with workplace problems through manipulation and unhelpful office politics."[2]

Before you make your next leadership hire, ask yourself if this person has the talent required to succeed in the role you are about to entrust to him. If you hesitate for *even* a moment, keep looking. You'll be glad you did.

Lack of Passion

Passion is a strong feeling of enthusiasm about or for something. It's something that others can sense, and it cannot be faked. Yet every day, leaders come into the office after pumping themselves up with a

Starbucks beverage in an attempt to present themselves as energized and connected. Everyone can see right through them by 10:00 A.M. as the caffeine high begins to wear off.

Then there are those of us who have worked for a boss whose passion for work came alive just around quitting time. Assignments were given as the boss walked joyfully out the door, while we got to put in the overtime needed to get the work done. A good boss needs to be passionate about his job all day long if he wants his employees to feel the same and give their best performance. The thing you need to know about passion is that it's contagious!

Failure to Live Up to Promises

Imagine what it must be like to work for someone who keeps making promises yet never fulfills them. Apparently, it's more common than we think. According to a 2007 Florida State University Study, two out of five bosses don't keep their word.[3]

I can only think of a handful of acceptable reasons to break a promise you made to one of your employees. I'm not saying that things don't happen or that something might legitimately get in the way of you keeping your word. Your actions after the promise is broken will determine what happens next.

For example, I find that most leaders hate confrontation. Rather than telling an employee why they are not able to keep a previous commitment, they instead pretend as if they never made the commitment at all. They figure the employee will forget about it, which is rarely the case. If you are unable to keep your word, at least have the courtesy of telling your employee why this is so. Many will stick by your side, as honesty is something that a lot of people are looking for from their bosses—and, as you've heard, it's in short supply these days.

Poor Communication Skills

It's hard to meet your boss's expectations when he hasn't fully communicated them to you. How do I know this? Because I once worked for a boss who told me the following: "You are not meeting my expectations, although I'm not sure I ever told you what they were." She had gone to Harvard, where perhaps they taught Mind Reading 101. I attended Northeastern University, which did not offer this course. Needless to say, our relationship ended soon thereafter, much to my relief.

It's impossible to have a good working relationship with a boss who has poor communication skills. Workers never know where they stand, nor do they have all the information needed to be effective in their jobs. Leaders with poor communication skills make bad bosses and have difficulty retaining staff.

Rather than trying to fill management roles in a hurry, employers would be better served if they slowed down and were more attentive in assessing communication skills before making job offers to managers. By doing so, they can dramatically reduce the number of Teflon managers they hire.

Micromanagement

Employees are stressed out trying to please bosses who watch their every move. I recall working for a boss who was a micromanager when I was employed as a temp. My boss made the assumption that I had very little in the way of education, as I was working as a temp doing administrative work in between jaunts to Europe. He kept standing over me and giving me detailed directions for logging accounts payable information. I tried to allow him his due, until one day I could no longer be silent. I said, "Vijay, you don't have to worry about me getting these entries right. I have an MBA." The look on his face was priceless and, thankfully for me, we laughed about it together. I never saw him look over my shoulder again. I can only imagine what it must feel like to experience this situation daily without the escape valve offered by my temporary work status.

Micromanagement is a costly management style that causes stress and employee dissatisfaction and stifles innovation, which ultimately impacts productivity and results in high employee turnover. Remember this the next time you catch yourself standing over your employee's shoulder.

Failure to Offer Opportunity

A report by Deloitte titled *Deloitte Study-The Global Human Capital Trends Report, 2016* noted that *demographic upheavals* have made the workforce both younger and older, as well as more diverse.[4] Millennials now make up more than half the workforce, and they bring high expectations for a rewarding, purposeful work experience, constant learning and development opportunities, and dynamic career progression. While more mature workers may not necessarily be vying for the corner office like their younger counterparts, this certainly doesn't mean they are happy remaining in place until they choose to retire.

Here's the thing: if you don't provide your workers with opportunity to grow and develop, someone else will. Take note of where your people desire to go and do whatever you can to help them get there, even if that means helping them find work elsewhere. They'll be sure to tell their friends what a great boss you have been, and who knows, one of those people may actually reach out to see if you'd be willing to hire them.

Outrageous Demands

Some managers don't understand that their employees actually have a life outside of work. I was one of those people. Twenty-four years old and single, I had no kids, and work was my life. I thought that was how everyone lived. I made ridiculous demands on my people to stay late and work on weekends. What the heck was I thinking? I wasn't, and eventually I saw the light when people left to pursue "better career opportunities"—code for, "I'm getting the heck away from you and taking my life back."

I'm sharing this story with you in case your demands are causing your best people to flee. If for some reason my behavior reminds you of yours, then I encourage you to do what I eventually did—get a life outside of work!

Lack of Attention

There was a recent news story about a guy in Spain who didn't show up for work for six years and no one noticed. Somehow, he managed to remain on the payroll without ever coming to work. While this might seem like a far-flung example, many workers can relate. They wonder whether anyone would notice if they failed to show up for work. Few would go as far as to try out their hypothesis, but if they are feeling this way then they are disconnected from their boss and, most likely, the company.

Make it a point to check in frequently with your people, especially your remote workers. Let them know that if they went away tomorrow, they'd most certainly be missed.

Jerky Behavior

Ever wonder why movies like *The Devil Wears Prada* are so popular? In the movie, Meryl Streep plays powerful magazine editor Miranda Priestly, clearly the boss from hell. Many people can relate to having a boss who has flames coming out of her nostrils. When I had a boss like that I spent my evenings in meditation classes just so I could make it through another day. It wasn't until I decided that I'd rather spend my evenings taking salsa lessons that I finally decided enough was enough.

Things are different today. Most people don't live in fear of losing their jobs and not finding another, nor are they worried about getting a reference from their boss because, in my experience, most will be gainfully employed elsewhere before the boss throws her next temper tantrum. There is no longer any point in being a jerk at work—that is, unless you are solopreneur and you enjoy treating yourself badly.

Fear-Based Leadership

Some people might put this under the category of jerk alert; however, I'm choosing not to because I believe that fear-based leadership isn't necessarily about being a jerk. It's about insecurity. Some leaders haven't quite grasped the concept of creating an atmosphere where employees do what they are asked because they want to, not because they feel they have no other choice.

Not all employees will depart as a result of fear-based leadership. Those who remain will be the weak people who don't have the strength to go elsewhere, which may be a worse scenario than one in which everyone has departed.

Lack of Backbone

If a leader isn't going to stand up for his people then why would you expect his people to remain in a one-sided relationship? Imagine making a mistake under the direction of your boss, and then being reamed out by his boss while your boss stands there quietly. That would only have to happen one time before most of us would resign.

If the boss isn't able to stand up on behalf of his employees, chances are he isn't standing up for the team either. No one wants to work for the weakest link in the company. Most will bail.

Lack of Feedback

I once coached a CEO who didn't do performance reviews because he was concerned that his employees wouldn't like him if he gave them feedback. I told him that it didn't matter whether his employees liked him. They needed to respect him, and they certainly weren't feeling respect for him as they huddled in their cubicles wondering if they were going to be receiving a raise or their walking papers.

Employees want and need feedback. If you don't give it to them, someone else will.

Management by Numbers

Leaders who manage by the numbers—basing every decision on how it will impact the bottom line—often forget to add the people element into the equation. Here's the real bottom line. People aren't driven by profits. They are driven by an emotional connection with the person they report to and by a feeling of purpose, a sense that their work is valued. Remember that the next time you are tempted to run the numbers before honoring an employee's request.

The True Cost of Employee Turnover

Some people think that employee turnover is simply part of the cost of doing business. These are the same people who view employees as disposable assets. When asked about the cost of employee turnover, they'll spout a formula that sounds something like this: one or two times an employee's salary. I don't believe these numbers, and nor should you. The true cost of replacing an employee varies by company and position. If you are going to use employee turnover as a metric for magnetism, then you need to know how much it *really* costs when someone leaves.

I first introduced my Employee Turnover Calculator in my book *Talent Magnetism: How to Build a Workplace That Attracts and Keeps the Best*. People who have used this tool have told me that the results have given them pause. You can fill in the blanks in the form below or use my free online Employee Turnover Calculator (on my website, matusonconsulting. com) to have the numbers automatically tallied for you. Of course, if you are a magnetic leader you will seldom need to use this tool, or even give the matter a second thought, as it's rare that anyone voluntarily leaves you.

Costs of a Person Leaving

Employees who have announced their resignation have already begun to transition out of the company. While working out their notice period, their full attention is elsewhere. Others in the organization are picking up the slack, which prohibits them from giving full attention to their own jobs. In addition, consider the following costs:

Situation	Actual Cost
The cost of the employees who must fill in for the person who leaves before a replacement is found	
The fees for temporary help or consultants needed to fill in while position is re-staffed	
The cost of the time spent by manager or executive for exit interview with the employee to determine what work remains, how to do work, why employee is really leaving	
The amount of money the company has invested in the departing person's training; the cost of lost knowledge, skills, and contacts that will depart with employee	
Cost of lost customers the departing employee is taking with him (or that will leave because service is negatively impacted)	
The increased cost of unemployment insurance	
Separation pay	
Subtotal	$

Hiring Costs

You might get lucky and find a candidate through a referral from a friend, but most likely you'll need to post and advertise the position. Consider the following hiring costs.

Situation	Actual Cost
The cost of advertising, internet posting, employment agencies, search firms, employee referral awards	
Increase in starting pay, as salaries have risen since you last hired; bringing everyone else in the department up to market rates	
Cost of time spent screening resumes, arranging interviews, conducting interviews (by both HR and upper management), checking references, and notifying candidates who were not awarded the job	
Fees for assessment testing, background checks, drug screening (usually done on more than one candidate), and time spent interpreting and discussing results	
Cost of time spent assembling and processing new hire paperwork, explaining employee benefit programs, and entering data to ensure employee receives a paycheck	
Subtotal	$

Training Costs

It would be great if all employees arrived fully trained, but this is not usually the case. Things are done differently in every organization so you must factor in the following costs.

Situation	Actual Cost
Cost of new employee orientation or onboarding	
Cost of specific training for the person to perform his job, such as computer training, product knowledge, company systems	
Cost of time spent by others to train the new person and money spent on outside training to ensure the new employee is able to do her job	
Subtotal	$

Loss-of-Productivity Costs

Because new employees do not enter a job completely proficient, it will take time before they are fully productive. Factor in the following productivity costs.

Situation	Actual Cost
Cost of time the manager spends directing, reviewing work, and possibly fixing mistakes	
Cost of errors not caught by manager	
Loss of good will as the company scrambles to preserve its relationship with valued customers and clients	
Plummeting employee morale as overworked employees assume more responsibility while the new hire is being trained	
Cost of turning away new business, as the company focuses on stabilizing	
Subtotal	$

Tally your subtotals to determine the true cost of losing this employee.

Categories Associated with Turnover Costs	Subtotals of Actual Costs
Costs of a person leaving	
Hiring costs	
Training costs	
Loss-of-productivity costs	
Total cost	$

Whether you actually take the time to calculate the cost of employee turnover, you now have a better sense of the effect Teflon leaders are having on your organization. Teflon pans were all the rage back in the day, before concerns about the toxic chemical emissions took hold. The same holds true for Teflon leaders. For years, we didn't pay much attention to the toxins these leaders were emitting into the organization and the impact it was having on the health of the workplace. We now know the damage these people can do, and we simply cannot afford to turn a blind eye to this growing phenomenon.

Why Leaders Should Have Term Limits

The office of the president of the United States has term limits. Leaders in organizations should have term limits as well. Here's why.

You May No Longer Be Right for One Another

I've always said that if I had come over on the *Mayflower*, I would have felt compelled to head west after my work was done setting up the colony. That's because I'm a strategist. I don't enjoy routine work, nor am I particularly good at it. A lot of leaders are like me. They may be the right person at a certain point in the business. However, they may no longer be the best person to have in a leadership role, or in any role, as business needs shift.

You're Breathing Your Own Exhaust

If you've ever worked in an organization where there is rarely change in leadership, then you understand how stifling it can be. When leaders remain in place forever, there is no room for fresh air or new ideas. Rotating leaders out of the organization allows new people to come in and energize the company.

You've Got Leaders Who Have Retired in Place

We all know people who have stayed with an organization because it was easier to do so than it was to leave. These individuals do their jobs and nothing more. They usually fly under the radar screen and try not to get noticed. This is a problem, especially if the leader heads a team of people who want to be noticed for their own contributions. Do yourself and this leader a favor: agree when his term will be up and take steps to find a new leader who is excited to take office.

We have come a long way since Teflon pans, and hopefully you've come a long way as well. However, I have to admit that I may have a few of these pans sitting in a drawer somewhere, as they bring back memories of happy times in the kitchen with my family. I've moved on, though, and have invested in new cookware that produces better (and safer) outcomes. I encourage you to move on as well. Hunt down those Teflon leaders who are hidden away in your organization. Although you may have had some happy times together, Teflon can be toxic and can do more harm than we'd originally thought. Treat yourself to a new and improved set of leaders who have the stickiness required to operate successfully in today's business environment.

Next, let's explore why employee engagement is not all it's cracked up to be and what you should be doing instead.

Gravitational Pull Exercise #3

Do a cost analysis of what employee turnover is costing your company. Is there significantly more employee turnover under one leader than under another who holds a similar position? Is there a common theme regarding why people are departing? Take preventative action to avoid further erosion of talent.

Notes

1. Nolan Feeney, "Millennials Now Largest Generation in the U.S. Workforce," *Time*, May 11, 2015, http://time.com/3854518/millennials-labor-force.
2. Gallup, "State of the American Manager: Analytics and Advice for Leaders," April 2015, http://www.gallup.com/services/182138/state-american-manager.aspx.
3. Brent Kallestad, "2 out of 5 Bosses Don't Keep Word," *LiveScience.com*, January 7, 2007, http://www.livescience.com/9488-study-2–5-bosses-word.html.
4. Deloitte, "The Global Human Capital Trends Report, 2016," http://dupress.com/periodical/human-capital-trends/.

Chapter 4
A Transfusion for Employee Engagement

Employee engagement, an employee's willingness to go above and beyond the call of duty, is in an anemic state, measuring a measly 32.5 percent in the United States, according to Gallup.[1] That means that, as a statistical probability, the majority of your employees don't give hoot about your company or your customers. Yikes! It's frightening. Yet companies are spending billions of dollars to increase engagement in their organizations, clearly to no avail. Continuing to do more of the same to improve engagement isn't going to move the needle. What we need instead is an infusion of magnetic leaders who can inject higher levels of commitment into the workplace.

Why Employee Engagement Programs Don't Work

Employee engagement programs *don't* work. Companies keep trying to buy the love and affection of their employees. This approach may appear to work in the short term; however, all you have to do is look around to see that there is always a bigger boat or better free food very close by!

Companies all around Silicon Valley are trying to outdo one another with outrageous perks and enviable compensation packages. One Silicon Valley company that is not playing this game is Rocket Service, an organization that partners with software companies and helps them build out their online software. "Our mentality isn't to lock people in," notes Rob Castaneda, CEO of Rocket Service. Castaneda wants people to remain in his employ because they want to, not because they feel they can't afford to leave.

Castaneda, a father of three young children, makes it a point to leave the office to coach some of his kids' various sports. "I never sneak away. I want the team to see me leaving to coach my kid's team so they will do the same." He goes on to lament how disappointing it must be for the children of parents who have all these great perks but who are unable to leave the office to see their kids' school play or baseball games. "I see the nannies dropping the kids off at sports and picking them up," Castaneda says. Eventually, these people will realize that the wealthiest people on the planet aren't the ones with the fat paychecks and outrageous perks; they are the ones who have discretionary time. Actually, given the engagement scores, we can assume that many of them may have already come to this conclusion.

The Employee as a Free Agent

Back in the 1950s and 1960s, employees typically remained with one employer throughout their lifetime. This is clearly not the case anymore. A U.S. Bureau of Labor Statistics' report released in January of 2014 shows employee tenure in the United States to be, on average, 4.6 years.[2] According to the report, the median tenure for workers 25 to 34 years old is 3.0 years, compared to the median tenure of workers ages 55 to 64, who had a median tenure of 10.4 years. Some industries, like tech, tend to employ a greater percentage of younger workers, which means companies in these industries must maximize talent as soon as it comes through the door. It's time to treat people like free agents. This means that you have to demonstrate daily why an employee should choose you.

Woo Your Employees Every Day

One thing that is very clear these days is that employees no longer feel an obligation to remain with the same employer. The "I'm here, until I'm not" mindset is prevalent in employees at most businesses. In fact, the idea of giving two weeks' notice no longer seems to be standard practice, especially among workers who feel disengaged.

Magnetic leader Ron Bryant, president of Baystate Noble Hospital, believes that it's his job to make the people around him successful: "I empower people. I really believe if people feel they are part of the organization and setting their own direction, they will enjoy coming to work every day." Bryant goes on to say, "I try to make people successful, rather than having people try to make me successful. I have to create the environment where they can be successful. I always ask, 'What can I do for you?'"

Leaders like Bryant understand that they have to demonstrate to their employees every day that they are worthy of their leadership role. They have to woo their people daily. The day you decide to take off may be *the* day your employee receives a call from an agent (also known as a headhunter) who has an irresistible opportunity. If you are treating your employees as well as you treat the people you are trying to convince to come work for you, then you can rest assured that your employee will dismiss the agent's request. If not, you may as well kiss this employee goodbye.

Five Questions to Keep You on Track

Most of you reading this book have enough on your plate, and you may think I'm telling you that you should be doing more. That's not what I'm saying. You don't have to do more; you have to do better. For some of you, that might mean sharing some of your own responsibilities with team members, so they can grow. For others, it might mean checking in on a more formal basis so your employees feel more connected. All of you will benefit from being more intentional in your efforts to create the kind of connections that spark magnetism. Here are five questions you should ask yourself frequently to ensure you stay on track.

1. **Am I fully present or merely going through the motions?** I'll be the first to admit that there are times that I'm having a conversation with my teenage daughter or son when I'm not really present. I'm thinking about what I'll make for dinner that evening or how my husband and I will split up so we can attend two parent meetings at school that are scheduled for the same time. Or worse, I'm reading my e-mail while my daughter tells me about her day.

   I observe leaders going through the motions all the time. A top executive may be in the middle of what seems like an important meeting when someone who appears to have a lot of clout walks into the room. In midsentence, the leader turns his attention to this new person, thereby signaling that the conversation he was originally having isn't all that important. Or I see a leader who is texting while his employee is asking him for feedback on a particular project.

Nothing says, "I really wouldn't miss you if you disappeared tomorrow" more than a leader who is not present when engaging with his people. Every now and again, ask yourself if you were really present when an employee asked for a few minutes of your time and you granted his request. If the answer is no, go back to the employee and apologize. Then take steps to make sure you don't repeat this behavior, even if it means leaving your phone in your desk drawer so you aren't tempted to multitask when you should be paying full attention.

2. **Am I shining the light more on my people than on myself?** I've worked for some leaders who always started their sentences with "I" rather than "we." After a while, we employees recognized that our only role was to serve this leader. We put up with this situation, as we were in the middle of a recession and we were happy just to have a job. Today, this "me" style of leadership can result in online shaming or the crew conducting a full-scale mutiny, as people have plenty of choices, including boarding the next boat that comes by or throwing the captain off the ship.

Sam Reese, CEO of Vistage, a peer-to-peer membership organization for CEOs, says it best: "A lot of leaders think it's about themselves. Every now and again, a leader like this will join a Vistage peer group. He or she thinks they are the only one in the business who knows what they are doing." It doesn't take long for other group members to show them the error of their ways. "When someone calls you on your behavior, you then have an opportunity to turn their feedback into something of value," Reese says.

Think about this the next time you are tempted to prove you are the smartest person in the room. Resist the temptation to take credit for the work of others and instead give credit where credit is due. When you shine the light on others, it reflects brightly on you.

As the hospital president Ron Bryant points out, magnetic leadership is about making your people look good. Bryant knew early in his career that he wanted to be a leader and he also recognized that he could build strong relationships. He understood the importance of giving enthusiastic credit to hard-working team members and that a humble attitude would take him a lot further than a reputation as a hotshot.

3. **Would I want my son or daughter working for someone like me?** Every generation hopes the next generation has it better. Is your leadership style the kind that you hope your son or daughter will experience? If you were to hire your child, would he or she be proud to call you boss? If you think the answer is no or maybe, then you've got some work to do.

   Some of you may be working in family businesses and may have your children reporting to you. If you are feeling confident (or brave), ask them: If they had to do it again, would they choose to work for you? If they say they are unsure, ask what changes you need to make to get an immediate response of "Of course!" the next time you ask.

4. **Am I worthy of those who have entrusted me with their careers?** Not a day goes by that Kevin Washington, president and CEO of the YMCA of the USA, doesn't think about serving his people and his community. "I'm trying to create an atmosphere where people can thrive." Washington says. "You need to give people a pathway where they can shine. This includes giving them the tools they need to be successful."

   Career development is at the top of the list of what younger job seekers look for from their employers. As a leader, you hold the key to the development of your people. You can keep the purse strings tight and tell people you don't have the budget to support their career aspirations, or you can step up to the plate and give the career development of your team high priority. You can be the kind of leader who sees potential in people before they see it in themselves, or you can insist that your employees stick to their job descriptions—in which case, you risk being in a state of perpetually training new people, as your team members keep exiting the back door. The choice is yours. Of course, you already know which side I hope you choose!

5. **What can I do today to improve by 1 percent tomorrow?** I believe that improvement comes with effort. If you improve a little bit every day, you'll make significant shifts in no time. You have to start somewhere, however.

   Begin by making a list of all the things that you, as a leader, are good at. Now put a check mark next to those items for which improvement would move you forward a mile rather than a mere inch. Next, write down specifically what you will do tomorrow and the next day and the day after in order to advance. Don't filter yourself or let anyone else tell you that something is impossible. Use this list as your compass. Stay the course, and I guarantee that you will improve your leadership ability substantially in no time. Your efforts will not go unnoticed, as word spreads quickly when a leader is as great to work for as you are.

How Work Is Killing Employee Commitment and Profits

I entered the working world at a time when it was considered normal to leave the office by 5:00 P.M. Of course, there were the occasional projects that might require employees to stay late or come in on the weekend. However, this was the exception rather than the rule. Flash-forward to today, and employees are expected to be available 24-7 or to work a shift on a moment's notice. Many employees are sleepwalking through the day because they worked all night, leaving innovation and growth at risk, as well as profits.

Many in the older generations complain about millennials because they are bucking the trend and refusing to stay late simply because it's expected. I've interviewed hundreds of millennials as part of the work I do for clients, and I hear one thing over and over again: "Don't mistake my ability to get things done quickly as laziness." Millennials don't understand the concept of face time, nor do they understand why they should be punished for completing work more efficiently than their more mature coworkers. They feel that if their work is done, why shouldn't they leave and attend to matters that make them feel whole? I applaud them, as I wish I had been that brave when I was their age.

Many companies are failing to adapt to the needs of the generation that is now the majority in the workplace—millennials. Failing to accommodate the new ways of working that the younger generation demands will result in your company being left behind and eventually becoming irrelevant. Case in point: I was having a conversation the other day with the U.S. president of a global company that has just acquired a 50 percent share in a company considered much hipper than the parent company. He told me that he recognized the need to adapt the parent company's culture to mirror that of the acquired company, which is filled with millennials, who represent the future of the workplace. He also said he was having a difficult time convincing his senior management team that this needed to be done. He's not giving up the fight, however; he made it very clear that the parent will be leaving its new partner alone, as interference would most likely do more harm than good to that business.

Unrealistic Expectations

During the recession, employers cut their workforces to the bare bones. For many, that mindset hasn't changed, in spite of the fact that business is booming. Some companies are trying to maximize revenues by maintaining recession levels of staffing even though business has improved considerably. Other companies are having a difficult time filling jobs. The pendulum has swung, and there are shortages of qualified workers in some fields as well as lots of competition in terms of hiring.

Simply put, employees are exhausted. They are often required to do the work of two people, yet their performance and pay remain the same. I don't see how much longer this can go on before we see a significant impact on productivity and profitability.

It's time to throw your recession mentality out the door. You'll never grow by cutting back. Take a look at your headcount and make sure you're adequately staffed given the level of service you aspire to provide to your customers and your plans for business growth. Do this today.

The Open Office Environment

I spent eighteen months of my career in a cube, and I can tell you they were the most unproductive eighteen months of my life. I could hear the guy next to me loud and clear (and I do mean loud), and I had a difficult time concentrating on tasks that required complex thinking. People popped their heads up, like gophers, to chat at the most inopportune times, and I knew more about the state of my coworkers' health and marriages than I ever wanted.

It's time to close the door on the open office environment. Let's just say it was a great social experiment and leave it at that. It's difficult to remain committed to the task at hand when distractions are all around you. People are wearing headsets for privacy, which defeats the idea that people should be in open cubes so they'll collaborate more.

Companies are working every day to create offices that look more like McDonald's playgrounds than workplaces, yet employees are still miserable. It's time to stop playing games and get back to work, so that people are free to leave at a reasonable hour and get their lives back. Don't believe me? Ask your employees what they prefer. But do so only if you are prepared to hear their answer and make changes.

24-7 Leadership

I get that we are working in a global economy, yet there are still many people who work in positions that don't require collaborating with fellow employees or helping customers in different time zones. Asking everyone to be attached to smartphones, on call 24-7, is just dumb. It's also unsustainable. Younger workers, many of whom are living at home, will think nothing of leaving an employer who subscribes to this model without a valid business reason for doing so.

Give your people a break. Resist the temptation to send out an e-mail at midnight because you had something you wanted to get off your chest before you went to bed. Encourage your team members to set boundaries as well. By doing so, you'll be sending the message loud and clear that being a workaholic is not something that you or the organization values. And while you are at it, encourage people to take time off to recharge their batteries.

My philosophy on work-life balance aligns closely with that of Basecamp CEO Jason Fried. We are both on a mission to change the way work works. Fried states publicly that he doesn't want people working more than a forty-hour week on a sustained basis. At Basecamp, four-day summer workweeks (of eight-hour days) are the norm, and, my personal favorite, one-month sabbaticals are awarded every three years. In addition, employees get three weeks of paid time off, and those with one year or more of service receive a general Basecamp holiday gift—in 2015, it was a choice of visiting one of sixteen amazing locations around the world, paid for by the company. Employees with less than one year's tenure receive a more modest gift; in 2015, the holiday gift was a night out on the town. The company changes the holiday gift every year to keep the element of surprise alive. Don't bother reaching out to Fried about a job, though; people rarely leave his company. I'm sure you don't have to ask why that is so!

I'll admit that some of the practices that Basecamp has instituted may be easier to do when you are privately owned. However, there is much here for larger companies and nonprofits to note. It really comes down to creating the kind of workplace where employees love to work and customers love to do business. If you don't know what this means, then ask (notice that I didn't say survey) your people what they value most and consider their answers before you spend more time creating policies or benefits that are so yesterday.

Egocentric Leaders

Self-centered leaders create a dynamic at work that is in direct opposition to what workers are seeking. It's hard to feel fully satisfied with your work tasks and conditions when your boss is focused entirely on herself. An "I care about you; now let's talk about me" mentality creates dissension among the staff and destroys any trace of employee commitment.

People don't work for companies. They work for people. This is why the idea of servant leadership—a philosophy in which leaders put the needs of their people before their own needs—has become so popular. For some, servant leadership may seem like a radical concept. These are people who should *never* be given the privilege of leading others. For the rest of you, this philosophy of leadership is a good reminder of what you need to do daily: put people before profits so that employees feel well cared for. In return, your employees will care for your clients in the same manner that you care for them. When you achieve this state of leadership throughout the organization, profits will soar.

Too Much Talk of Engagement

I remember walking into a church in Rome with my young children and hearing a voice from above saying, "*Silencio!*" My then seven-year-old daughter looked up at me and asked who was speaking in such a commanding voice. I told her it sounded like God. Okay, maybe it wasn't God, and years later we did have a pretty good laugh at my response. However, the message was clear: silence in the church.

I wish I had a recording of that voice so that I could play it back every time the words "employee engagement" are spoken. Years ago, we talked about employee morale. Today we talk about engagement, which is a fancy word for morale. Companies are dropping billions to achieve this state of nirvana. I believe it's time to stop spending money on this hoax, and instead focus on something that works—magnetism. I've remained by the side of some bosses solely because of their magnetic leadership. They sought my advice, demonstrated to me that I mattered, and encouraged me to spread my wings and grow. They certainly didn't throw money at me in order to get me to stay or feel motivated, nor did they keep asking me to wait until the annual survey before I provided them with feedback regarding my experience at work.

The Simply Magnetic Organization

So now that I've convinced you to stop focusing on employee engagement, what should you be doing instead? I'm proposing that you begin to focus on what matters most—purpose and humanity.

Let's begin with purpose. Your purpose is what you stand for and the reason your organization exists. Most employees today are seeking a deep connection to the work they do. They are looking for purpose. They want to know specifically how their work makes the world a better place. If you don't give them a strong sense of purpose, someone else will. Most companies have a purpose, but it's often not stated in a way that connects with employees emotionally. For example, you may be one of the many companies publically stating that maximizing shareholder value is your purpose. I'm here to tell you that making money is not a purpose. It's an objective, and it's one that is hard for the average employee to wrap his head around.

I know this firsthand, having worked for a financial consulting firm whose purpose was to make the owner wealthier. I had a hard time engaging my head and my heart around this goal, and couldn't wait to find an employer with a purpose I could connect with.

As chief purpose officer at the professional services firm Pricewaterhouse Coopers (PwC), Shannon Schuyler's role is to activate the firm's purpose, which is to build trust in society and solve important problems. Schuyler believes the firm has to substantially change the way it manages people as millennials become an ever larger part of the company's workforce. Purpose must be front and center. "Millennials want to make sure the time they spend doing something has value. There has to be meaning," notes Schuyler. Belief in, and an understanding of, the company's purpose helps employees draw a line from the hours they spend doing a piece of the project to the project's overall value for the firm. PwC employees also want to know how clients translate the work that they do into better services for the clients' customers and employees.

"We hire eleven thousand students a year. In order to keep them, we need to remind them why they are important to us. This generation asks the why question," Schuyler says. "We have to answer the question, why I would be missed if I went away." Understanding the reasons their work is important is key for this generation; they need to know how everything fits together.

PwC takes purpose one step further than most and will soon begin embedding purpose into performance appraisals, asking managers to include examples of how employees have aligned their own work with the company's core purpose. The firm is also looking at ways to make sure its purpose is prominent in learning and development courses. And having an executive completely devoted to purpose indicates that the firm is indeed putting people and purpose before profits.

Intrapreneurship: A New Model for Employee Stickiness

Imagine being in a job where you have little control over how much work you are assigned or how the work will be done. Most people don't have to imagine this, as it is their reality. Lack of control over one's work is a huge stressor, and it is one of the reasons so many employees are disengaged at work. Who can blame employees in this situation if they are not committed to doing what's right for the customer? They're too busy slogging through another exhausting day to worry about anyone but themselves.

Now consider the flipside of this equation. You are working in a job where you feel you have a purpose. You get to decide how much work to take on and how the work will get done. For many of us, that means entrepreneurship. However, not everyone wants to run her own business, nor is every worker qualified to do so. But even when entrepreneurship isn't quite the right fit, people still want to feel more in control of their lives.

I advise my clients to embrace *intrapreneurship*, a practice that encourages employees to act like entrepreneurs inside organizations. This model is being adopted by businesses seeking innovation and dramatic growth. Perhaps you've heard of a few of the companies in the examples that follow.

Originally called the "awesome button," the Facebook Like button was first prototyped in one of Facebook's infamous hack-a-thons. In another organization, a manager probably would have written it off as a dumb idea. Not at Facebook. The company encourages employees to bring new ideas to the table and has created a work environment where employees feel comfortable sharing their ideas freely.

The Sony PlayStation, which put Sony at the head of the class in the fast-growing and highly profitable gaming industry, was created by Ken

Kutaragi, a relatively junior Sony employee who spent hours tinkering with his daughter's Nintendo to make it more powerful and user-friendly. A forward-thinking senior leader at Sony dismissed the grumblings of Sony bosses regarding the time Kutaragi was "wasting" at work and encouraged him to keep toying around with the unit.

I bet some of you are thinking, "I could never allow the people I have in my employ this kind of freedom." If that's the case, I suggest you take a closer look at the people you've been hiring and make adjustments accordingly.

Before you dismiss intrapreneurship as a fad, consider the following. *The Deloitte Millennial Survey,* released in January 2014, found that 70 percent of millennials see themselves working independently at some point rather than being employed within a traditional organizational structure.[3] Millennials want things companies aren't currently giving them: autonomy, creativity, and meaning. But if companies give their talent something to focus on, projects to own, and control over their own work, these valuable workers will remain with their employers and help move their company forward.

If intrapreneurship sounds intriguing to you, your next step is to ensure that you have an environment where intrapreneurs can thrive. This begins and ends with confident leaders who can ignite and sustain passion among team members.

Throughout part 1 of this book we've discussed the power of magnetism, which is something that many of us have experienced or have observed. Now that you are aware of the strong pull associated with magnetic leaders, it's time to transform your leadership style from "meh" to magnetic. The transformation begins here and ends with you. Let's get started.

Gravitational Pull Exercise #4

Write down the purpose of your company and department. Why are you in business, and if you went away tomorrow would anyone notice? Include purpose in your daily conversations with team members and clients.

Notes

1. Gallup, "Employee Engagement Is Stagnant in U.S.," January 13, 2016, http://www.gallup.com/poll/188144/employee-engagement-stagnant-2015.aspx.
2. Bureau of Labor Statistics, U.S. Department of Labor, "Employee Tenure Summary," September 8, 2014, http://www.bls.gov/news.release/tenure.nr0.htm.
3. Deloitte, "The Deloitte Millennial Survey," January 2014, http://www2.deloitte.com/content/dam/Deloitte/global/Documents/About-Dloitte/gx-dttl-2014-millennial-survey-report.pdf.

Part 2

*Irresistible You:
From Ordinary
to Extraordinary*

Chapter 5
Seven Irresistible Traits of Magnetic Leaders

I've met many leaders who possess what I call magnetic traits. You simply want to remain on the call or in the room with these people because of the connection you feel when you interact with them. This pull keeps their employees connected to them. Fortunately, magnetic leadership traits can be acquired. To really integrate the learning from this book and to make it part of your being, you'll need to allow yourself to be vulnerable. This means taking an *honest* look at your current style of leadership and being open to the possibility that you need to make minor improvements in some areas—or that perhaps a complete overhaul is necessary.

I know from my experience as an advisor to executives that dramatically increasing your magnetism on your own is difficult. We rarely see ourselves as others see us. If you need help, ask for it. Find an accountability partner—someone who will tell you what you need to hear and not necessarily what you want to hear. This partner might be a mentor, a peer at another organization, an executive advisor, or a coach.

I've identified seven irresistible traits of magnetic leaders. I'm sure there are more. The goal here isn't to have you go through the headings in this chapter and check off each box. Nor is it to provide you with a huge list that seems impossible to achieve. Instead, I want to provide you with a framework for what it takes to be a magnetic leader.

As you read through this chapter, think about what it means to possess these characteristics. Rate yourself on each trait using a scale of one to ten (with ten being high). Ask an accountability partner (and if you are really brave, your employees) to do the same. Compare your ratings. Do this quarterly until you've reached the level you feel your employees deserve from you, and then revisit this exercise semi-annually to ensure you maintain your allure. To help you, I've provided an evaluation tool, which you'll find at the end of the chapter.

Here are the seven irresistible traits of magnetic leaders, in no particular order.

1. Authenticity

Authenticity was one of the first words people mentioned when I asked them to describe what comes to mind when they hear the words *magnetic leader*. It's in the blood of all great leaders, and without it leaders will find themselves dead in their tracks. Yet authenticity isn't usually found on an interviewer's checklist when she is assessing candidates for leadership roles.

I first met Christie Smith at Deloitte University, where we were both attending a function. I immediately knew she was different, and I say that in a good way! She was authentic then and continues to be so today, even as she has risen in stature. Smith believes that authenticity is about your own journey toward self-actualization. "I'm true to myself," Smith says. "I embrace all that I am and the paths that I've taken and I'm willing to live that in everything I do. That creates followership. I take seriously the responsibility that followership brings. Making my people or clients truly great and opening up avenues toward their own journey is what I do."

Smith grew up the youngest of eight kids in what she describes as a competitive environment: "Our family disease was overachievement!" She goes on to say, "Sports and people were my gifts. My mother called me the Pied Piper. I never belonged to a clique in school. I've also learned over time that humility is seeing yourself as who you are, both good and bad. I've fully come into that phrase in the last ten years. I'm really clear about what I'm good at and what I'm not good at." Employees tell Smith that she is unlike any leader they've ever worked with. I believe if I had experienced a leader like Smith, I would still be in the corporate world working for that person. On second thought, maybe it's a good thing that never happened.

You can't mention the word *authenticity* without the word *trust* coming up too. That's because you can't have one without the other; people naturally trust those who are authentic. According to the 2016 Edelman Trust Barometer, one out of three employees, globally, does not trust the company for which he works.[1] And we all know that companies are not animate—they are legal entities. It's the people in charge who are receiving failing marks. In Japan, Russia, and France, the situation is far more ominous, as employee trust levels hover below 50 percent. Clearly, leaders across the world have some work to do.

Building trust has never been more important or more challenging. It takes effort to build trust. While once upon a time a boss may have been trusted based merely on her position, this is no longer the case. Too many managers act with their own self-interests in mind, causing their employees to mistrust them, and their actions are shared widely on social media channels by employees who seem to have no filters. What may have been a small issue a decade ago can now turn into a full-blown crisis overnight. Don't even get me started on the impact the recent surge in tell-all books by former employees is having on the trust factor in the employer–employee relationship. This leads me to some ways leaders can build a deep, trusting relationship with employees.

Admit You Don't Know Everything

"I used to think the CEO knew everything and told everyone what to do," says Eileen McDonnell, chairman and CEO of Penn Mutual, a mutual life insurance company. "I've learned that it's important to surround yourself with good people." The people you oversee deserve the truth from you, including the fact that you are also a work in progress.

My mentor Alan Weiss always says he learns more from those who attend his programs than the participants learn. He's probably one of the smartest people I know, yet he is still learning every day. Here's what he says about personal improvement: "If you improve 1 percent a day, in seventy days you'll be twice as good." Let your 1 percent improvement today be the idea that it's okay—no, it's actually a good thing—to remind those who work with you that you don't know everything and that you are looking forward to learning something new from them.

Be Truthful

The quickest route to building trust is to tell the truth, and that means keeping your word. Why do people find this so difficult to do? Lack of trust in business leaders is at epidemic proportions. In 2014, the public relations firm Edelman, in its Trust Barometer survey, gathered data from more than 33,000 respondents and discovered that 80 percent of people don't trust business leaders to tell the truth.[2] I don't believe most people wake up every day thinking, "Whom can I lie to today?" This lack of trust occurs because people hate confrontation and will do anything, including lying, to avoid it. We all know someone who was promised a raise or a promotion and then got nothing. Or we know people who were assured resources would be given to them, only to find out through the grapevine that those resources were allocated elsewhere. The worst offenders are those leaders who promise an employee her performance review on a particular date, and then that date goes by and nothing happens.

You may be thinking, "What the heck do you expect of me? I'm responsible for a ton of people and for getting our company's new product out the door in less time than it takes to make a donut." Great! That's all about you. Now what about the people you promised to care for when you asked them to join your team? They deserve a leader who keeps her word. I understand that things change, and the people who work for you understand that too.

However, here's what they don't understand: they don't understand why you simply can't be truthful. For example, if you learn an anticipated raise is no more, why not tell people the news immediately? Admittedly, the staff won't like the message. However, most will appreciate your honesty. They can then decide their next move. I'm betting they'll remain in your employ, as honesty seems to be in short supply these days.

Share Your Backstory

We tend to look at people who have risen to a certain stature in their careers, and we forget they weren't always at the top of the food chain. Many have overcome struggles we can't even imagine. The account of how a person got to his current position is called his backstory. Everyone has a backstory. Sharing their backstory is a way for leaders to make a deep connection with their people, which can lead to a more trusting relationship. Hotelier Henry Kallan shared his backstory with me, and shares it freely with others too. He emigrated from former Czechoslovakia at the age of twenty-one, with very little money in his pocket and no knowledge of English. He began his career in the hotel industry as a busboy. Kallan's passion for hospitality was fortified by a keen eye for detail and an exceptional instinct for how to make people feel comfortable and cared for. At the age of twenty-seven, he became the youngest general manager in New York City for the Gotham Hotel (currently the Peninsula). There are now six hotels in his collection, with a seventh on the way.

Kallan's backstory is part of his DNA. It's foundational to the way he shows up every day. After hearing his story and interviewing him for this book, I understand why employee turnover in his hotels is significantly less than it is for his competitors. Kallan believes people will do their best work when they feel secure in their jobs. His approach to leadership, which is deeply rooted in transparency, allows people to know *exactly* where they stand at all times. This kind of transparency is something every leader can strive for.

According to the 2016 Edelman Trust Barometer, almost eight in ten people say hearing information about a leader's personal values is important in building trust. Just as important is hearing about the obstacles a CEO has overcome, her success story, and how her education has shaped her. Now that you know this, think about your backstory and answer the following questions:

- What shaped your hopes and dreams from an early age?
- What obstacles did you overcome in order to get where you are today?
- What were some of your successes along the way?
- How did your education (or lack thereof) shape you?

Jot your answers down and make it a point to share your backstory with current and prospective employees. Watch carefully, as no doubt you will see the quality of your interactions change dramatically.

To increase authenticity, ask yourself the following:

- Do I bring my whole self to work or do I leave parts at home?
- What have I done within the last week to build trust?
- How often do I share my backstory with employees and prospective candidates?

2. Selflessness

Magnetic leaders put the needs of their people first. Kevin Washington, president and CEO of the YMCA of the USA, believes magnetic leaders don't sacrifice people for their own gain. As a result, they have a significantly stronger emotional connection with their people than leaders who put their own gains first.

Baystate Noble Hospital President Ron Bryant has also learned the importance of putting his people first. "Early on in my career, I wasn't like that," notes Bryant. "I try to make my people successful, rather than having people try to make me successful." To do this, you have to create an environment where people can succeed.

I had the opportunity to observe Bryant in action when he engaged my services to help align his leadership team with the ever-changing challenges associated with the health-care industry. It was his first time in the role of CEO, and it was a badge he wore proudly. I watched the way he interacted respectfully with his team and others. He was always in learning mode and he pushed his people to better themselves. He didn't do this to earn a bigger bonus. He did it because he knew his people had the potential to be better. It was in their best interest to develop their leadership skills, and by challenging them he was giving them an opportunity to excel and perhaps take on a larger role in health care.

I've worked with many leaders over the years, and I have to admit that Bryant is at the top of my list of favorites. He's a humble man who cares deeply for the people and the community he serves.

Being selfless is one of the hardest things you'll do as a leader. It's human nature to take the quickest path to fame and fortune. So what if you have to walk over a few dozen people to get there? It's the American Dream, right? Well, it's more like the American Nightmare if you're the person who is working day in and day out for someone else's success.

Millennials, in particular, aren't inclined to put up with leaders who climb over one another (and their people) so they can be King of the Mountain. These employees see right through selfish behavior. Keep this in mind if you are seeking to attract and retain this younger sector of the workforce—or any sector, for that matter.

Magnetic leaders serve their people. Bryant gets this. He makes it a point to always ask his people, "What can I do for you?" When is the last time you asked that question of someone on your team? When you do, make sure you listen to the answer instead of waiting to talk. If it's been longer than two days since you asked, make today the day. Put the question on your calendar daily until it becomes habit.

Look at your followers and ask yourself:

- Are people following me because of what I can do for them or are they doing so because of what I can do *to* them?
- Do I take more than I give?
- What have I done today to put others before myself?

When you first ask yourself these questions, you may not care all that much for your responses. That's not necessarily a bad thing. It's like getting on the scale after not having weighed yourself for a long time. Many of us do so with trepidation, for fear of what we might see. However, taking that one tiny step is often the impetus to make essential changes for a long and healthy life. The same holds true when you stop to reflect on your actions as a leader. Maybe you aren't thrilled with how you're doing right now. But that doesn't mean you have to continue down the same path. Think for a moment about what you'd like your legacy to be. Do you want to be known as the person who served his people well or would you prefer to be remembered as that crappy, selfish boss a former employee is now writing a book about?

3.   Strong Communication

Magnetic leaders are strong communicators. When they speak, people listen. Martin Luther King Jr. was quite a magnetic leader. His "I Have a Dream" speech is a great example of the power of communication. King's words still bring tears to people's eyes, and it's been more than fifty-three years since he delivered this speech. He spoke from the heart, which allowed him to connect with his followers in a memorable way.

How often do you find yourself filtering your words when addressing your staff? Stop that! Let your team experience the real you. Remember authenticity? I do. When I was younger and living in Houston, I would dial back my communication style in an attempt to closely mirror my peers and to fit in. Picture a gal from New York speaking in a gentle manner and using a Texas twang. It's hard to keep a New York attitude in check, and the real me often showed up, resulting in confusion and mistrust. I quickly learned to adjust my communication style without pretending to be someone else. I was fortunate to have had a mentor who helped me understand that it's not just what you say, but how you say it. Language is everything, which is a lesson I still carry with me today. Think about this before entering into a conversation with your employees. Choose your words and tone wisely.

I know there are leaders who subscribe to the idea, "If you don't hear anything from me, everything is fine." This is one of the worst things you can do to your people. Why? People need and want feedback.

Employees are asking for feedback, and employers are turning a deaf ear to those requests. When you fail to communicate with people, they come up with their own stories. Studies consistently show that employees are seeking more communication, or shall I say clear communication, from their leaders. Yet this is still an area where leaders are failing miserably. Gallup's 2015 *State of the American Manager* study found that consistent communication—whether it occurs over the phone, electronically, or in person—is connected to higher engagement. For example, employees whose managers meet with them regularly are almost three times more likely to be satisfied at work than employees whose managers never hold regular meetings with them.

This same study found that employee commitment is highest among employees who have some form of daily communication (face-to-face, phone, or digital) with their managers. Managers who use a combination of face-to-face, phone, and electronic communication are the most successful in engaging employees. And when employees contact their manager, engaged employees report their manager gets back to them within twenty-four hours.

While communication regarding work is important, Gallup has also found that employees are more connected to their leaders when those leaders demonstrate interest in their employees outside the workplace. A simple handwritten note congratulating an employee on his engagement or a call home to see how an ailing child is faring can make a lasting impression.

Magnetic leaders make it comfortable for employees to share what's going on in their lives, whether the matter is work related or not. They understand that there is no such thing as work life and home life: we have one life, and we are doing our best to live life fully.

Here are some questions to ask yourself as you look to increase the effectiveness of your communication skills:

- Am I *fully* present when people speak?
- Is my communication clear or is it a bit cloudy?
- How often have I reached out to team members in person, on the phone or via e-mail or Skype this week?

4. Charisma

Entrepreneurs Dan Kenary, cofounder and CEO of Harpoon Brewery, and Rob Nixon, PANALITIX CEO, both cited charisma as a trait that is common among magnetic leaders. As a leader, you ask people to take a leap of faith and join you on a journey. Charismatic leaders are artists who paint a picture of what that journey might look like, inviting others to step into the frame—and they do so in a way that is irresistible.

A charismatic leader influences and inspires others. I would place Greater Boston Food Bank CEO Catherine D'Amato in the charismatic leader category. I've watched her speak at venues where there was standing room only and I've also observed her discussing strategy with her senior leadership team. What strikes me most is the feeling you get when she is in the room. She gets people to take action without ever asking them to do so. When she speaks, people listen—they don't want to miss a single word she says.

Some people are born with a natural charisma. However, charisma can be acquired and magnified in a few ways.

Exuding Confidence

It's hard to gather a following without confidence. Would you follow someone who wasn't quite sure where he was going? Of course not! Those who appear confident put others at ease and build trust more easily than those who don't. Decide on a path and move forward confidently.

Recent studies suggest that confidence is also related to dress. According to an article in the *Wall Street Journal* titled "Why Dressing for Success Leads to Success," wearing nice clothes may raise one's confidence level.[3] A joint study by the Yale School of Management and the *Journal of Experiential Psychology* in 2014 found that in a mock sale of a hypothetical factory, participants dressed in suits were less likely to give up ground than those who were negotiating while wearing sweats. The suits wound up selling their hypothetical factory for almost $2 million more than their casually dressed counterparts. Still think dress in the workplace no longer matters?

Expressing Positivity

I can't think of many charismatic leaders who are negative people. That's because positivity attracts people, while negativity turns others off. Positivity is something that we seek to surround ourselves with. D'Amato's inner belief as to what is possible is contagious. You can't help but follow her lead as she works to end hunger.

Positive leaders empower others, which is something you can certainly learn to do. Give people an opportunity to shine. Allow your employees to determine the best way to get things done. Provide encouragement along the way and acknowledge them when the assignment has been completed. There. See how easy it is to empower people?

To increase your charisma, ask yourself:

- Do I genuinely like being around people?
- Do I express my ideas in a way that exudes confidence or do I radiate self-doubt?
- Do I expect people will do their personal best or do I believe most people will merely look to get by?

5. *Transparency*

Candor and transparency go hand in hand. "The problem that I see with managers is that they have a self-preservation mentality," notes Broughton Hotels CEO Larry Broughton. This attitude dramatically impacts managers' ability to be transparent. For example, their department may be overstaffed, yet they won't let others know about the situation, nor will they offer to share resources on a temporary basis, for fear their kingdom will diminish in size. This instinct for self-preservation is quite common in organizations. It's also contagious, as hiding the true situation becomes a learned behavior. This conduct significantly impacts productivity and profitability.

"We are in the relationship economy," Broughton says. "People want to do business with people they know, like, and trust." Nowhere is this more evident than in the consulting business. The other day I had a prospect ask me if I had experience putting together compensation plans. I told her I had limited experience and that I could bring in a compensation expert to work with me if need be. I could have easily hedged her question. Instead, I chose to be transparent. She appreciated my candor and quickly agreed that we needed to find a way to work together.

As leaders, we have to develop a culture where people aren't afraid to be honest and real. This begins with you. The next time you're in a situation where you are tempted to sugarcoat things, take a pause. Think about the message you are about to deliver. Is it crystal clear or a bit murky? Adjust accordingly and then say what you need to say. Employees crave transparency, just like you probably do. Treat them the way you'd like to be treated, and I promise you they'll give you and your customers all they've got.

To increase transparency, ask yourself the following questions:

- How often do I filter what I tell people?
- How frequently do I shield information from others for my own benefit?
- Am I being transparent or a bit murky?

6. Vision

Magnetic leaders are known for their ability to create a shared vision, and they tend to look at the world through a different lens than most people use. For example, instead of asking the question "Why?," they ask, "Why not?" Nonprofit CEO Catherine D'Amato has told me that she can see the actual outcome—whatever it is she wants to happen—in her mind's eye. She's is always pushing the envelope, which leads to innovation. "We have a lot of innovation of thought here at the Food Bank. How you deliver a service and be more helpful to people allows their life to be better," notes D'Amato.

One of the talents of Service Rocket CEO Rob Castaneda is his uncanny ability to see potential in people before they see it in themselves. Perhaps that's because he's open to people contributing in different ways. Castaneda told me how he tapped an employee who was working in HR, and told her that he thought she would be more challenged in marketing. She was resistant at first but finally relented. As Castaneda expected, she has taken to the role and is doing superior work. "I ask people where they want to go and if they have the ability to do more," states Castaneda. "That's a lot more telling than the resume that says, 'here is the resume written down as I think you want to see it.'"

To assess where you are on the visionary scale, ask yourself the following questions:

- Am I focused on everyday tasks or long-term outcomes?
- How often do I take time out of my day or week to think about the future?
- Who in the organization has potential that is not being realized and what can I do to help unleash that potential?

7. Resilience

Surprises are the new norm, and resilience is the lifeline of leaders. Leadership requires the courage to confront uncomfortable realities, the faith that there will be a solution when one isn't immediately in sight, and the resolve to carry on in spite of the feeling that the situation is hopeless.

Broughton, a Special Forces veteran, knows about resilience firsthand. The major event for him was the market downturn in 2001. "Before the downturn, I was flying high and making lots of money," he recalls. Soon after he had $84 in the bank and a wife who left him with a six-month-old baby. "I realized that I had to change," he said. Broughton refused to take failure as an answer. Today, he runs a successful full-service hotel management company and employs seven hundred people.

I doubt there is even one leader who hasn't been thrown off his horse at some point in his career. It's what you do when you are faced with a fall that determines how the rest of your story unfolds. I've been thrown off my horse several times and admit that my first inclination was to stay on the ground. I soon realized that I needed to pick myself up, examine what went wrong (and right), and pull myself back together. Thankfully, I live in America, where second and third chances are all around. I've come to realize that I cannot control everything around me. I can, however, control how I choose to handle things. I've learned that it's better to fail than to not have tried. I've also learned to fall forward.

To build resilience, ask yourself:

- Do I take responsibility for my failures or do I place the blame elsewhere?
- Do I pick myself up quickly after a failure and move forward?
- Do I play it safe to avoid failure or do I take risks so I can grow?

Magnetic Leader Self-Assessment

Here's the evaluation tool that I promised you earlier in this chapter. I placed it at the end of the chapter so you wouldn't be tempted to check off the boxes too quickly and move on to the next chapter without a clear understanding of magnetism and why it really matters.

MAGNETIC LEADERSHIP INDIVIDUAL SELF-ASSESSMENT _Please rate yourself in each of the following areas:_	_Ratings_ _4 = All the time_ _3 = Most of the time_ _2 = Sometimes_ _1 = Rarely_ _0 = Never_ _N/A = Not applicable_
Authenticity	
1. I bring my whole self to work.	
2. I do something to build trust weekly.	
3. I share my backstory with employees and prospective candidates on a regular basis.	
Selflessness	
4. People follow me because of what I can do for them rather than because of what I can do to them.	
5. I give more than I take.	
6. I regularly put others before myself.	
Communication Skills	
7. I'm _fully_ present when people are speaking to me.	
8. I communicate in a clear and concise manner.	
9. I frequently reach out to team members in person, on the phone, or via e-mail or Skype.	
Charisma	
10. People like being around me.	
11. When I express my ideas, I exude confidence.	
12. I believe people do their personal best and therefore manage accordingly.	
Transparency	
13. I filter what I say before speaking.	
14. I shield information from others for my own benefit.	
15. I'm _completely_ open when communicating with staff, peers, and my boss.	
Vision	
16. I see things with my mind's eye long before others do.	
17. I regularly take time out of my day or week to think about the future.	
18. I recognize potential in others and make it a point to help them achieve their greatness.	

MAGNETIC LEADERSHIP INDIVIDUAL SELF-ASSESSMENT Please rate yourself in each of the following areas:	Ratings 4 = All the time 3 = Most of the time 2 = Sometimes 1 = Rarely 0 = Never N/A = Not applicable
Resilience	
19. I take responsibility for my failures.	
20. I pick myself up quickly after a failure and move forward.	
21. I take risks so I can grow.	

© Matuson Consulting, 2016. All Rights Reserved.
Any area with a score of 2 or less requires immediate attention!

Now that you know what it takes to achieve magnetic leadership status, let's move on to how you can leverage your attraction to pull top talent toward you.

Gravitational Pull Exercise #5

Complete the Magnetic Leadership Individual Self-Assessment. How did you fare? Make note of those areas in which you scored a 2 or lower. Jot down some ideas about how you can improve your ratings and achieve magnetic status.

Notes

1. Edelman, "2016 Edelman Trust Barometer: Annual Global Survey," http://www.edelman.com/insights/intellectual-property/2016-edelman-trust-barometer/.
2. Edelman, "2014 Edelman Trust Barometer: Annual Global Survey," http://www.edelman.com/insights/intellectual-property/2014-edelman-trust-barometer/.
3. Ray A. Smith, "Why Dressing for Success Leads to Success," *Wall Street Journal*, February 21, 2016, http://www.wsj.com/articles/why-dressing-for-success-leads-to-success-1456110340.

Chapter 6

The Force of Attraction: Pulling Top Talent Toward You

The other day, I was speaking with an executive who was getting ready to uproot her family, yet again, and make a move back across "the pond." Like most parents relocating with kids in tow, she was lamenting the impact this move would have on her family. She then confided in me that she was taking the new assignment because she was asked to do so by a leader with a strong pull. She had worked for this gentleman before and simply could not pass up the opportunity to do so again. I joked around with her and said, "He must be one heck of a magnetic leader," to which she replied, "Yes, he is!"

Magnetic leaders like the one I just described are rare—and this woman knows it. Here she is moving her family back to Europe, after having moved them from Europe to the states only a few years earlier. I sincerely doubt she would have even considered taking the assignment if the person making the request had been more ordinary than extraordinary. That's the power of magnetism. It's the pull that people feel when a magnetic leader makes a request. It's so strong that you cannot help but say yes when asked to agree to a new assignment or a new job opportunity that will allow you to work for the magnetic leader again.

Rob Nixon, CEO of PANALITIX, uses his magnetism to pull in talent seamlessly. "I'm able to attract talent when others are unable to," he notes. "Team members do not want to be managed—they're adults, not children. They want to follow inspiration, energy, and vision. If you have that, then people want to be around you." Nixon says he has no problem hiring the best people he can find. "People want to be part of something great," he says. And if you've ever seen Nixon make a presentation, you know there is a heck of a lot of greatness going on in his head, heart, and company.

In the last chapter, we talked about the connection between magnetism and charisma. From what I see, many leaders tend to dial down their charisma in an effort to conform to social norms. But when it comes to attracting talent, this is a huge mistake. Think about it. Most people are attracted to the sizzle. Here's what I mean by this. You're in a restaurant and you've settled on the meal you are planning to order. Out of the corner of your eye, you note an amazing sizzling dish go by. Suddenly, all bets are off. You tell the waiter, "I'll have what he's having."

Let's take a look at how this plays out in the workplace. You are working for a low-key boss who does little to inspire you. Out of the corner of your eye, you notice another boss who always seems to be interacting dynamically with her people. You start to second-guess your choice of bosses. You see an opportunity to have what everyone else in that department is having, and you're first in line the moment a position in this person's department becomes available.

It's not difficult to stand out in the crowd these days, especially when it comes to attracting talent. You just have to be willing to be bold and filter out the advice that the masses are giving you.

Recruitment Is Dead: What You Should Do Instead

I know everyone is telling you to go onto LinkedIn and post, "I'm hiring!" However, everyone is wrong. These days, my LinkedIn feed resembles my experience walking down the cobblestone alleyways in the Latin Quarter of Paris, where restaurants have their hawkers shouting on the streets, trying to pull you into their bistro or café. It seems like everyone in my alley on LinkedIn is yelling, "We're hiring!" They are wasting their breath, as it's impossible to be heard with all the noise on this channel. Besides, why should someone answer the call of a stranger when her real friends and colleagues are knocking on her door daily with a buffet of job offerings?

Recruitment is dead. There, I said it. Here's why. To be hired by most companies, you have to be a long-distance runner (because it takes so darn long to hit the finish line) and an accomplished hurdle jumper (because there are a ton of barriers you have to jump over in order to win the job). Who needs that, especially in a hot job market where there are more employers in the race for talent than candidates?

I'm even hearing from recent college grads how overwhelming it is these days to navigate the hiring landscape. It's like taking a trip to Baskin and Robbins and having thirty-one flavors to choose from. Most people are happy with the standard restaurant offerings of chocolate, vanilla, or strawberry. Anything more and they get stuck. That's one of the reasons that magnetism works so well for leaders looking to staff open positions.

Most people don't know many magnetic leaders, so it's doubtful you'll have all that much competition in attracting people to you, if you are indeed magnetic. Magnetic leaders really don't have to exert a lot of energy when they are seeking talent. Why? Most have a line of people waiting outside their door, all wanting to work for them.

Okay, maybe you're still working on getting your magnetism to a level where your pull is attracting people to you, and perhaps you are not quite there yet. Here are some ways you can pull talent toward you while also increasing your allure.

Speak Everywhere

The other day, I had the pleasure of seeing Catherine D'Amato, CEO of the Greater Boston Food Bank, speak at an association meeting. Her keynote was about her journey to becoming a food banker. The room was filled with talented people in an industry D'Amato has hired from. During her presentation, she encouraged audience members to explore their passion. She suggested they reach out to others in the room and request an informational interview. She then shared that she had hired the majority of her executives this way. Most had come to her to learn more about what it was like to work for a nonprofit. She encouraged people in that audience to reach out to her as well. Knowing D'Amato, this was an authentic offer; in addition to being the CEO of the organization, she is also its ambassador.

I thought more about her proposal and realized that inviting people to reach out to you during a speech is a wonderful way to pull top talent toward you while increasing your magnetism. The opportunity to get to know someone in an informal setting can be a game changer. You have a chance to gain much more insight than if you were to sit across the table from that person in a formal interview. In return, giving people access to you, without any expectations, can really help to increase your appeal.

Connect with Customers

"We always look for talent in our own user base," notes Jim Pickell, president of HomeExhange.com, a company that helps like-minded travelers swap homes and experiences. "People who have done exchanges really just get it. When we bring people in from the outside, it can take ninety days to a year to onboard people who aren't familiar with our user base," states Pickell.

I can see why this talent strategy works so well for a business like Home-Exchange.com. Pickell is easily attracting like-minded people to join a company they already feel passionate about. He's tapping into his followers and giving them an opportunity to join the travel revolution. I can also see why this approach may not work for everyone, as the last thing you want are clients thinking you are poaching their people. An alternative is to simply ask your client if he knows someone, perhaps a friend or relative, who might be looking for a new opportunity. With any luck, he'll say yes and will then offer to connect you with this person.

Be Visible on Campus

No, this doesn't mean that you should set up a booth at the college fair. That's what people who are recruiting do. You don't want to work that hard for what will most likely be a small return on your investment. Here's what you want to do instead. You want to find a club on campus that aligns well with what your company does. For example, if you are CEO of a marketing firm or you head up a marketing department, you want to connect with the leaders of marketing clubs on college campuses that are either close by or in an area where you frequently travel.

Keep in mind that magnetism is also part of the relationship economy. That means that you are looking to build long-term relationships that will help to feed your talent pipeline.

Now that you've identified the schools and the clubs that are most appropriate for you, reach out to the people who lead these clubs and offer to sponsor events. This may mean supplying the pizza for the weekly meetings, or you may be asked to come in and speak with members of the club regarding career opportunities. Remember tip number one, *speak everywhere.* This is part of the talent magnetism strategy that will yield results for years to come. And while you are on campus, be sure you get to know the dean and professors, so that when you are in need of entry-level talent you can pick up the phone and ask your contacts for some names.

Former Biogen CIO Raymond Pawlicki built some very strong relationships across college campuses. Not only was this an effective recruitment strategy; he told me that he really enjoyed connecting with students who would soon be part of the workforce. Pawlicki's pull was so strong that he was able to fill jobs when others couldn't.

Be a Talent Maverick

The United States has 5.4 million job openings, according to the February 2016 JOLT's report put out by the U.S. Department of Labor,[1] and an unemployment rate of 5 percent, which means we are pretty much at full employment. In order to survive and thrive under these conditions, you have to take control. You can no longer sit by passively waiting for your HR team to deliver candidates to you. You have to pull out all the stops and attract candidates to you.

HR departments simply don't have the capacity to fill all of the job openings in most companies. In addition to recruiting, they have a ton of other work to do. You also have to stop relying on technology like the Applicant Tracking System (ATS), which seems to be part of everyone's application process these days, and instead go back to the basics. Why? Because many great candidates are getting lost in the ATS black hole and are never found again. Here's a case in point. A friend of mine was an experienced baker who had applied for work several times at a local co-op. She was never called for an interview. Soon after she told me this I happened to be shopping at the co-op, and I ran into the bakery manager, who mentioned in passing that he was in need of a baker. I knew he had at least one good candidate in his line of sight—only he could not see her. The person in charge of the ATS had never forwarded her resume to him.

Again, I'll remind you that we are all in the people business, as most companies are unable to operate without people. Let's get back to basics and start inviting people in to have a conversation rather than making sure they cannot penetrate the walls that we ourselves have built to keep people out in an effort to make our lives simpler. So what does this mean to the talent maverick? It means that you do whatever you need to do to get people in the door, even if it means bucking the system.

Why Attraction Trumps Recruitment Every Time

Just in case you aren't totally convinced of the ROM (return on magnetism) at your disposal, here are some things to consider.

You Don't Need A Lot of People When You Have A Lot of Talent

People who are talented usually shine in more than one area. This means you can shift talent around in your organization when business needs change.

Talent attracts talent. Remember when you were a kid and you were standing there waiting for the team captain to select his team from the pool of students waiting to hear their names called? If you were like most kids, you hoped and prayed you'd be asked to join the team with the most superstars. Not all that much has changed since our days on the playground. Great people want to work with other great players. The opposite is true as well. If you allow slackers to remain in your employ, don't be surprised if you begin to see your superstars defecting to another team.

Less Effort Leads to Better Results

When you get to the stage where people are coming to you, you'll see how much easier it is to fill positions. You'll also notice a dramatic difference in the quality of people you are now able to hire. Why? Some of this has to do with you and your confidence. You'll be more inclined to pass on mediocre candidates because you know they are no longer your only choice. You'll also have a better understanding of the idea that talent attracts talent.

Magnetism Lowers the Cost of Talent Acquisition

Think about the actual costs you incur when you go into recruitment mode to fill a job opening. How much of an investment is required to actively recruit a new employee? For some, this may mean the cost to post jobs, paying for a booth at a career fair, the dollars you need to invest traveling from one college campus to another to recruit entry-level talent, what you pay each recruiter, etc. Of course, we can't forget about the recruitment fees many of you are paying to third-party recruiters, which can be as high as 30 percent of a candidate's beginning annual salary.

Now think about what it costs when someone comes to you and says she'd like to work for you. To be fair, an investment is required here as well. There is the time you spend meeting with this person (perhaps a few hours) and the coffee or lunch you may wind up buying, should you decide to meet outside the office. You may also add in the time you spent and any associated costs required to get your name out there (e.g., speaking at conferences, on campus, etc.). Clearly, you can see how attraction is *significantly* less costly than recruitment. And for most leaders, it's a lot less drudgery and a heck of a lot more fun.

You Can Ignite Passive Candidates into Active Candidates

Passive candidates are those people who are employed and are not looking for a new opportunity. For reasons I can't quite figure out, many employers are much more interested in passive candidates than active candidates. Perhaps it's the thrill of the hunt. Be that as it may, in an economy where there is a severe shortage of workers who are actively looking for new opportunities, one must tap both sources.

Imagine for a moment that you are one of these passive candidates. You are fairly content in your job and you have no real interest in making a change right now. You get a call from a Dan in HR or a headhunter asking if you'd be interested in learning more about a job opportunity at company XYZ. It's the third call like this you've received today. You say no as quickly as you can, and you hang up. Now consider the following scenario. You receive a call from a VP who is known as a really cool guy to work for. You've heard nothing but great things about this person. In fact, you saw him speak at an association dinner last month and, quite frankly, you were blown away. You left the meeting thinking, "If I ever look for a new job, this would be the guy I would call." Somewhere along the way, this leader caught your attention. His magnetism has created an irresistible pull. You've gone from passive job seeker to active job seeker, without even realizing it. He'll have no problem bringing you into the fold.

Success Breeds Success

It's human nature. We all want what someone else has. Last week I was speaking with my client Wendy Foster, executive director of Big Brothers, Big Sisters of Massachusetts Bay, and we were discussing how success breeds success. I've been advising Foster and her team on their talent strategy. You know how difficult it is for businesses to pull in talent these days. Now imagine what it's like for a nonprofit that's not in a position to shower employees and job seekers with the latest extravagant perk to hit the scene or salaries that used to be reserved for people with law degrees. The team has elected to follow my recommendations and is going after a sector of the workforce that most are ignoring—stay-at-home parents who are looking to get back into the job market. Specifically, those who wish to work part-time from home. Foster said to me, "All we need to do is pull in a few of these people and they will no doubt bring others with them." I couldn't agree more.

As her team moves from recruitment to attraction, they will have more time to focus on their mission, which is to provide children who lack positive adult role models with strong and enduring, professionally supported one-to-one relationships with caring, responsible adults who change their lives for the better. If you are a parent, you know how strong the parent network can be. One parent tells another parent about a product, service, or opportunity and, in turn, that parent tells ten other parents. This network is even stronger these days due to the sudden surge in online parent portals and blogs. I suspect it won't be long before the team at Big Brothers Big Sisters of Massachusetts Bay experiences success in their efforts to attract the right talent to their organization, and this success will, in turn, breed more success elsewhere in the organization. I would be remiss if I didn't add that this success all begins with Foster, whose magnetism has attracted me and others to her organization and has gotten us all to stick around!

Magnetic Leaders Give People a Reason to Stay

How many people do you know who are voluntarily leaving magnetic leaders or magnetic companies? In chapter 4, I talked about magnetic leader Jason Fried, founder and CEO of Basecamp, and I mentioned the fact that he rarely has a job opening in his organization. (We'll go into more detail about retention in chapter 10.) It's been my experience that people who are pulled into organizations by magnetic leaders are much more likely to stay than those who've been recruited to join the company. I found that this was so because magnetic leaders tend to be good at building relationships. These relationships are what really keep employees from being pulled away by forces that, quite frankly, can be very attractive, such as the promise of more pay, an exciting assignment, or a lofty job title.

Of course, there are many benefits to having people remain with your organization, including being known as a place where people really like to work. That reputation alone can be a huge differentiator when it comes to attracting top talent. Why? Because most people really don't enjoy the whole job search process. Can you blame them? If they are going to put forth the effort it takes to consider a new position, they'd like to know that there's a good chance they'll be happy at their new home and they won't have to go through the job search process again anytime soon.

How to Avoid Being a Best-Kept Secret

I know a lot of great leaders who are quite humble. Few people outside their inner circle are aware of who they really are or what they've done, both professionally and personally. These same leaders complain to me about how hard it is to attract talent these days. I tell them that they absolutely must pump up the volume. The only other choice is to wither away in the background while their peers take the lion's share of the talent pool. Most immediately ask, "How loud do I need to turn it up?"

When I teach leaders how to toot their own horn so they can be heard in a sea of cubicles, I talk about what I call strategic bragging. This is where I encourage leaders to casually insert into the conversation something they are proud of that others don't know about them. It can be something personal, such as being a two-time Olympic medalist, or it can be something business related, such as a prestigious overseas assignment for a previous company, to open up a new market for the business. I then teach them how to introduce this personal accomplishment into a business conversation that, at first glance, may not have anything to do with their accomplishment.

This process of strategic bragging should be adopted by leaders who are looking to pump up the volume. Begin by asking answering the following questions:

- What awards have you ever won?
- What were the most significant outcomes you achieved in your corporate life?
- What are one or two personal accomplishments you are most proud of, but that most people don't know about?

Here are some things to keep in mind when working through this exercise. Do not filter yourself. In other words, do not second-guess what you are putting on your list because you think it may not be all that special. Most likely, it is. I mentioned the two-time Olympic medalist because that leader didn't think that having two Olympic medals was all that special—until the group I was facilitating knocked some sense into her, that is! Now that you've written your answers down, take what you are most proud of and mention it in your bio, your LinkedIn profile, and conversations you may be having with team members and prospective employees.

Here's how this might play out. In the following scenario, the person who is sharing his experience came to the United States twenty years ago and spoke no English. He is having a conversation with Ben, a guy he'd like to have come work for him. "Ben, I understand it can be a bit scary to leave someplace where you feel really comfortable. I, too, did this more than twenty years ago. I came to this country and did not speak a word of English. I left what some would have considered a fairly good job to give my family a better life. Taking that risk changed my life for the better. My hope is that you will be able to say the same thing, as a result of taking a chance and coming to work for me." Now compare this to what most hiring managers say. "Here are the job duties and our expectations. Do you have any questions?" Need I say more?

The way to make sure you are not a best-kept secret is to make yourself visible. You do this by building a strong personal brand, including strategically bragging, whenever the opportunity arises.

How to Get Others to Push Talent Toward You

You are thrilled with your dentist or your child's pediatrician. Whenever anyone you know is in need of a doctor, you are the first to chime in with a recommendation. The same thing happens in business. There are people whose names come up whenever someone asks, "Who should I contact regarding a job?" Be sure the name they give out is yours. I understand that your first instinct might be, "I don't want to waste my day talking to people I can't help." You need to shift your mindset. You can and should help them. Taking fifteen minutes out of your day to speak with a person may end up being the best fifteen minutes you've invested in a long time. That person may wind up being exactly the type of person you are looking to hire. If not, she may know someone who fits the bill perfectly. She will be a walking advertisement for you. She will tell everyone how great you are for giving her the time when many people wouldn't. This one small move will strengthen your brand as a magnetic leader.

Stay in touch with your peers and let them know when you are on the lookout for talent. Be as specific as possible about your needs so they can refer talent to you. Now you may ask, "Why on earth would they do that?" Think about it. One of your peers is asked to interview someone, as a favor to a friend. The person being interviewed is a great candidate, but your peer doesn't currently have any job openings. She doesn't want to disappoint her friend, so she refers the candidate to you, knowing that you are in need of an employee with this skill set. This will not happen if you don't make a concerted effort to stay in touch with your peer network.

As you can see, the key to pulling top talent toward you is strong relationships. Take time out of your weekly schedule to build relationships with referral sources, prospective candidates, and peers who work in other companies. If you commit at least one hour a week to doing this, it won't be long before you are known around town as *the* person people need to reach out to before making their next career move.

Now that you have a line of people outside your door waiting to work for you, let's discuss how to create irresistible hiring practices that will ensure you can pull these people into your orbit.

Gravitational Pull Exercise #6

Open up your calendar and select dates and times (a total of one hour a week) to build relationships with referral sources, prospective candidates, peers in other companies, and customers. Be specific. Jot down the names of the people you will reach out to and how you plan to connect with them (e.g., over lunch, coffee, etc.).

Note

1. Bureau of Labor Statistics, U.S. Department of Labor, "Job Openings and Labor Turnover," February 16, 2016, http://www.bls.gov/news.release/pdf/jolts.pdf.

Chapter 7
Irresistible Hiring Practices

You know from your own experience, and from that of your peers, that it takes time and effort to create the magnetism needed to pull talent toward you. For our purposes, let's assume you've been successful in your efforts to draw people in. You're halfway home. To cross the finish line, you'll need to sustain their interest in coming to work for you and your company, as you put them through the paces your firm requires before candidates are hired.

As you read through this chapter, I'm going to challenge you to look at your hiring practices every step along the way. Try doing so from a job seeker's perspective. Think about what areas you can improve upon. What steps can you eliminate? Are your hiring practices enabling you to hire the right people, or are they doing more harm than good? Let's begin by putting you in the driver's seat.

Take the Wheel

When it comes to hiring, magnetic leaders always remain in the driver's seat. They never delegate this task to someone else because they believe, like I do, that hiring is the most important job of any leader. Those who don't think this is so are probably the same people who keep complaining about the quality of their hires.

You can't delegate relationships, which is what hiring people is all about. The hiring process is essentially a matter of getting to know the candidates so that you can determine whether they are the right fit for your company, and vice versa. Now, I know that in some parts of the world arranged marriages are quite common and that some of these marriages do indeed work. But just because this is true doesn't mean that most of us would be better off having someone else select our mate. The same holds true with regard to the hiring relationship. In many cases, we spend more time with the people we work with than we do with our families. My experience tells me that I know best what will work for me in terms of a team member. I also know that no one can sell me like I can sell myself. And no matter what you believe, when you are hiring someone you *are* in the sales business. What I mean by this is that you have to take your candidate through a series of yesses, with the final being, "Yes. I'd love to accept your offer. When can I start?"

Here's the part that gets confusing to me. Many managers are fine delegating the hiring function to their assistant or someone in HR—that is, until this person is unable to fill the job as quickly as the manager expects. HR is doing its best to keep up with the hiring demands placed upon it by the organization and a very demanding labor market. Most HR departments simply don't have the bandwidth to keep up with today's hiring needs. To win the race for talent, you must take the wheel—take control of the situation.

Here's what I recommend to my clients who are looking to accelerate their ability to fill job openings with quality hires. Pick up the phone and personally call the candidates, especially those you are looking to source from another company. Right then and there you are sending a clear message to the candidate. You are letting him know that you are invested in the hiring process and that this is a priority for you.

Having someone else making the calls to candidates sends a message to them as well; however, the message may not be the one you intended to send. Nonetheless, candidates are free to interpret the calls any way they choose. Most will assume they are one of many people being called that day, and in some situations they might be right. Those who are gainfully employed and somewhat satisfied at work probably won't bother to return the call. Why? It's likely that they are receiving such calls daily. Like I said, take the wheel and make the calls yourself. And once you have the wheel, don't turn it over to anyone else until you've crossed the finish line.

Put the Pedal to the Medal and Stay the Course

Most companies are taking way too long to hire people, and in the process they are losing great candidates to the competition. They are also losing something else—future revenue. The 2015 CareerBuilder Candidate

Behavior study highlights the high cost of a bad impression.[1] The perception among candidates is that employers aren't responsive during the hiring process, and the results are staggering. According to the survey,

- 69% of job seekers say they are less likely to buy from a company they had a bad experience with during the interview process.
- 65% of job seekers say they are less likely to buy from a company they didn't hear back from after an interview.
- 58% of job seekers say they are less likely to buy from a company they didn't hear back from after submitting an application.

The hiring process matters—a lot! If you take away only one thing from this chapter, let it be that speed trumps perfection time after time. Here's what I mean by this. As you are methodically going through your ten-step hiring process, during which you are putting candidates through hoops that even you could no longer get through, your competition is throwing caution to the wind. They've collapsed their hiring process and are making job offers to the very same people you hope to hire. And I also hope you can see how important it is to get back to candidates. I recommend that you personally leave a message for those who've made it to the final round of interviews. Letters should be sent to everyone else. Please don't tell me that you can't afford to do this because you don't have the resources. Clearly, you can't afford *not* to do this!

The world of hiring, as we know it, has changed dramatically. For example, in today's mobile world it's not uncommon for an applicant to receive a job offer on her smartphone from another employer as she is leaving the parking lot after interviewing with you. She can certainly put an offer off for a day or two, but most cannot keep an employer at bay for the amount of time needed to go through a long, drawn-out hiring process. Most will take the offer extended rather than risk coming up empty-handed. With that in mind, here's how to cut your time to hire in half.

Keep Your Network Greased

You don't want to be in the uncomfortable position of trying to move forward from a dead standstill. Make it a point to check in regularly with people whom you'd consider hiring, should an opportunity become available in your organization. Do this quarterly by phone or over a coffee. Do the same with people who can refer you to those you might want to employ.

Cut the Excess

Make a list of everyone involved in the hiring process. Slash this list in half. There is absolutely no need for everyone on the team to interview the newest team member, unless, of course, you are running a democracy, which most organizations are not doing. And for goodness sake, if you have people interviewing their potential boss, stop doing this immediately. It's uncomfortable for the staff as well as the candidate, doesn't yield the results you think it might, and is not a practice I recommend employing. For those of you who are waiting for the candidate to be interviewed by a person who won't even be working directly with the new hire, I encourage you to move forward without that input. If you don't, the candidate will surely no longer be available when this person returns to the office or fits time into his schedule.

Collapse Interview Schedules

Hiring has to be a priority, so you need to look at ways to collapse your interview schedules. Be sure you have a team of people who are trained in interviewing candidates effectively, so you can quickly assemble an interview schedule for one day instead of over a three-day period, which seems to have somehow become the norm.

Think Ahead

You know without a doubt that you will need to check references. Instead of waiting until the end of the hiring process and adding more days to what may be already be a long cycle, why not start checking references as soon as it's clear to you that this person is a finalist? Sure, you may wind up making a few extra calls, but you also might discover some very interesting information about candidates that could be helpful in your decision-making process.

The "Disneyland" Approach to Talent

If you've ever been to a Disney park you'll know exactly what I mean when I tell you to "go left" when searching for talent. If you step back and watch all the people flooding into the park the moment the gates open, you'll notice a strange phenomenon. The majority of people will go through the turnstiles and turn to the right. There they will find crowds of people, long lines, and lots of frustrated visitors. Now, imagine if they had turned left immediately after walking into the park. The lines would be significantly shorter for attractions and food similar to those they are queued up for. A comparable thing happens in the hunt for talent. People follow the crowd when they should instead be looking for talent where no one else is looking.

Here's how to find talent where no one else is looking.

Try the Starbucks Strategy

I'm always amazed by how many people line up in the morning for their lattes with only one thing on their minds. Most don't give any consideration to the person who is making their drink, nor do they even acknowledge the person taking the order. If that sounds like you, then you are missing out on a huge opportunity to secure talent.

I've spoken with a lot of baristas, and most didn't grow up dreaming of whipping up coffee drinks. Nor did they count on graduating from college with a ton of student debt and few job prospects. What I'm saying here is that the person in front of you may be working in a coffee shop, in a retail store, or as a waitress in order to make ends meet. There is a pool of smart, well-educated, motivated people who are simply under-employed, and a job in your organization could be very attractive to these workers. Keep this in mind the next time you are waited on by someone who may very well make a great addition to your team.

Look for Those Who are Fifty, Fabulous, and Fired Up to Work

Where is it written that the moment you hit age fifty you are no longer fit to work? I wish I could say it's written only in a few places, but this certainly doesn't appear to be the case. Many employers are looking for that bright, shiny penny (also known as a millennial) to add to their head count. Don't be that manager. Instead, seek out mature workers to fill your job openings.

There are many benefits to hiring mature workers, including the fact that most won't be out partying on weeknights and will likely arrive at the office on time on a consistent basis. Their demands will be small. By that I mean, they'll be willing to forego the foosball table for a seat at the table. And I'd be remiss if I didn't mention that you will have a lot less competition trying to snag one of these candidates, since they are not in vogue.

Chase the Unemployed

If you've ever been unemployed, you know what happens. People stay away from you for fear that you have some sort of disease that will spread. Unemployment isn't a disease. It's a condition. If only employers would see it that way. That's exactly why I'm encouraging you to consider hiring the unemployed. In this group, there is an awesome subset of people, like stay-at-home moms and dads, who are looking to re-enter the workforce. For some it's been a while since they last held down a corporate job and they may be in need of a minor tune-up. Others, quite honestly, are re-entering the workforce with even more skills than they had when they left.

I know of a number of parents who have stepped out of the workforce while raising their families. However, this doesn't mean that they've completely stepped away from work. Some are running Parent Teacher Organizations (PTOs) with budgets bigger than yours, while others are volunteering at a number of nonprofits that are near and dear to their hearts. Many have become masters at fund-raising. The point is, you should not discount people merely because they've been out of the job market for a while. If you are the one who gives them the break they've been yearning for, they'll remain loyal to you for years to come. Can you say the same when you hire people who are gainfully employed?

Hire High-Potential People

My most successful clients surround themselves with people who, with time and additional training, have the potential to be as good, if not better, than they are. I applaud them for doing so. I'm not going to lie to you: it takes confidence to hire people who could someday do your job. But think about it. If there is no one to replace you, then you may be stuck in the same job forever! That thought is a heck of a lot scarier than the worry that one of your people is there to take your job.

What happens most often is that we hire a version of ourselves. The candidate we're drawn to may have gone to the same school that we attended or may have had a similar upbringing. Often, they closely resemble us in appearance. We could all learn something from the hiring process used by the Boston Symphony Orchestra (BSO). In 1952, the BSO pioneered what is now frequently referred to as blind hiring. Musicians auditioned behind screens so the judges couldn't see what they looked like, and they walked on carpeted floors so the judges couldn't determine whether they were women or men (the women often wore heels to auditions). This prevented the judges from making selections based on their own biases. As a result of this practice, the BSO increased the number of females it hired and more women began to show up for auditions. I know there are companies out there today trying similar strategies. However, they are still the exception.

I suggest you look to hire people who can add to the diversity of your organization. And when I say diversity, I don't just mean with regard to age, race, and sexual orientation, though that is important. I also am talking about hiring people who excel in areas that you do not and people who approach life in a way that is different from yours. By doing this, you'll stop the madness that seems to be spreading these days, which has leaders on the lookout for the 2.0 version of themselves.

You may want to follow Service Rocket CEO Rob Castaneda's practice of ignoring resumes and instead focusing on the person in front of you. What are his capabilities? Which areas does he excel in and where might he have potential? Does the candidate represent a sector of your customer base that you aren't fully exploiting? That's the sort of thinking that will allow you to take calculated risks that will pay off in spades. By doing so, you'll dramatically increase the number of qualified candidates for each open position. You'll also, no doubt, create a stronger team that can help you move into new markets.

People First, Jobs Second

What if, instead of trying to fill job openings with great people, you found great people and created jobs that would maximize their skills? This strategy has been a game changer for many executives, including D'Amato and Castaneda. Penn Mutual CEO Eileen McDonnell has her people constantly on the lookout for new opportunities for their talented employees. The company fills a third of its jobs internally. "We promote an environment for those who want to promote," says McDonnell. "I appointed a president and COO who is forty-one years old," she notes. "He started with the company as a college intern and has had sixteen different positions at Penn Mutual."

Imagine for a moment what might have happened if McDonnell had waited for employees to vacate their positions before moving the current president through various roles at this 169-year-old institution. In the mutual fund business, people tend to stay in their roles much longer than they do in the tech industry. McDonnell did something I tell my clients to do: provide opportunities for your talent to achieve their full potential before someone else makes them an offer they can't refuse.

I don't know when it happened, exactly, but somewhere along the line compensation systems were established to give organizations structure in terms of job titles and pay. This was done in an effort to provide hiring managers with guidelines so they could hire and retain team members. These very systems are now preventing leaders from attracting and retaining people. Most companies with formal compensation programs adjust their ranges annually, and when they do so, the ranges are adjusted to keep up with inflation. However, these adjustments don't take into account supply and demand, which is the driving force behind salaries. It seems kind of ironic.

It's time to go rogue. Many of your peers are already doing so. It's happening subtly—a bunch of winks and nods here and there enable executives to work around a system that no longer works. I'm glad they can do this, but what about the rest of the hiring managers in the organization who don't have the same political clout? Can they really get away with it? Probably not. Yet these are the very same people who are responsible for staffing the majority of the organization. These people must be unshackled so they can do their jobs.

The majority of compensation systems don't work given today's highly competitive recruitment environment. You'll have to either overhaul the system or throw it out and work in the here-and-now. I vote for the latter. Trust the fact that you've hired people who have good decision-making skills. (If you don't believe you have, then skip to chapter 11, where I provide advice on how to release employees who cannot release themselves.) Listen to your people when they come to you with the name of a person they think would be great for the organization. Work together to figure out how to best utilize this person's passion and skills and how to put together a compensation package that is mutually acceptable. Don't worry that they don't fit into any of those nicely crafted boxes on your org chart. Instead, focus on the results this person will help the organization achieve, as you continue to work toward attracting customers and profits.

Stop Requiring College Degrees

I can't believe I'm even saying this, as my husband and I are about to fund college educations for both our son and daughter, but here goes: stop requiring college degrees for those positions where a degree isn't really necessary. When you insist that workers have college degrees, your labor costs are artificially inflated, and at the same time the labor pool available to you is significantly decreased.

One of my clients is currently struggling with this issue. Her organization is affiliated with a national organization that requires degrees for jobs that most likely could be done successfully by non-degreed workers. In her case, these workers need strong communication skills. She's working slowly to change the requirement, but in the meantime she is struggling to fill specific jobs in a city where talent is extremely tight. Now I ask you, would you rather hire Candidate A, who doesn't have to rely on spellcheck before sending out a document, or would you go with Candidate B, who is a whiz at organizing events and can sell anyone on anything? Now what if I told you Candidate B doesn't have a degree? Would you discard her application?

There's a ton of evidence piling up about what's happening with actual learning on campuses these days, and much of it is not pretty. Drawing on survey responses, transcript data, and results from the Collegiate Learning Assessment (a standardized test taken by students in their first semester and at the end of their second year), researchers Richard Arum and Josipa Roksa concluded that a significant percentage of undergraduates are failing to develop the broad-based skills and knowledge they should be expected to master. They discuss these findings in more detail in their book, *Academically Adrift: Limited Learning on College Campuses*, and the results they describe are sobering.[2] The authors report that a large proportion of college students' gains in critical thinking, complex reasoning, and written communications are either exceedingly small or empirically nonexistent during their first two years of college.

Think about the results you want people to achieve and then sort out whether a degree is a "must have" or simply a "nice to have." If you can widen your net ever so slightly, you'll have way more candidates to choose from. I'd be remiss if I didn't tell you that when it comes to hiring talent, it's a numbers game. You can no longer be true to only one candidate. You have to have several "first" choices, as there is a good chance your top pick is also someone else's top pick. Remember my earlier advice to look for talent where others aren't? Expanding your search to non-degree holders is another example of this strategy. While others are passing up great candidates who may be shy a few credits, you'll have the opportunity to swoop in and grab some keepers for your organization. Give it a try. I doubt you'll go back to the old way of doing things. In fact, I predict you'll hunt for talent in places where, a year or two ago, you never thought you'd look!

You don't have to implement all of my irresistible hiring practices to experience success. Choose one or two, and embrace these new hiring practices. After you've mastered them, pick another one or two. If you are disciplined and fully committed to the new practices, I can pretty much guarantee you will see rapid results.

Now that you know how to fill your pipeline with quality candidates and you've made some swift hires as a result of your new hiring practices, you are ready to master the skills that will dramatically increase your gravitational pull and keep talent in your orbit.

Gravitational Pull Exercise #7

Write down the ideas that resonated for you in terms of looking for talent where others may not be looking. Draw up your battle plan so that you can attack that sector with force.

Notes

1. CareerBuilder, "2015 Career Builder Candidate Behavior Study," http://www.careerbuildercommunications.com/candidatebehavior/.
2. Richard Arum and Josipa Roksa, *Academically Adrift: Limited Learning on College Campuses*, Chicago: University of Chicago Press, 2011.

Chapter 8
Opposing Poles of Leadership: Influence in Action

You probably know people who seem to have been born with what I call the influencing gene. Regardless of what they do or say, they are able to move people to their side of the conversation. To the best of my knowledge, there is no scientific evidence that the ability to influence is actually part of our DNA. Luckily for most of us, influencing is a skill that we can learn. But before I share some ideas on how you can master influence, I want to talk about what influence is and what it isn't, as well as the relationship between influence and magnetic leadership.

Influence: What It Is and What It Is Not

Influence is asking for something you need in a way that allows the other person to say yes. For example, you may be working toward getting someone to say yes to a request you've just made—"Yes, I'll give you the extra head count you need." Influence is also about dissuading someone from taking action, or at least urging continued due diligence—"Do you think she is really the right person for this job?" "Shouldn't we at least look at several more candidates?"

Here's what it's not—manipulation. Many people mistakenly believe that when a person uses influence, he is trying to manipulate another. This could not be further from the truth.

Now, before we get too far along here, you need to understand that without trust there can be no influence. Think about this. How often have you honored a request from someone you didn't trust? The response from most of you is probably "never!"

Throughout this book, I've been discussing the connection between strong relationships and magnetism. If you've got a trusting relationship with someone, it will be that *much* easier to use influence to get that person to come work for you. The same thing happens when it comes to employee retention. Suppose an employee with whom you have a trusting relationship comes to you and tells you she is thinking of leaving the company. You believe that at this point in time, she would be making a mistake if she resigned. You tell her the reasons you believe this is so. There is a fairly good chance she will remain with you, because she trusts you to have her best interest in mind. Of course, you'd also tell her that the move was a good one for her if you honestly believed that was the case.

It can be challenging, as the CEO of a small company, to always do what's in the best interest of your people. Service Rocket CEO Rob Castaneda has found that when people have been with his firm for three or four years, they are really in demand. "Our mentality isn't to lock people in," states Castaneda. Sometimes you need to let people go so they can grow. "We always want people to feel like they can come back," he says. And the number of people who have blasted off and returned to Service Rocket is a testament to the fact that Castaneda means what he says.

Once again, the key is the trusting relationship that leaders like Castaneda and others have built with their team. When you have high levels of trust and you ask people to consider something, most will. And more often than not, they will honor your request. Think about this the next time you are trying to attract new employees or retain the ones you have. Approach discussions on matters related to attraction and retention as a conversation rather than as a challenge or adversarial dialogue. This small shift will yield big results. This is the power of influence.

Influence: Without It, There Is No Leadership

One of the most important parts of your job as a leader is to get your people the resources they need to do their jobs effectively. In every organization, you must be able to maneuver swiftly through the company so that you can best serve your people. Okay, let's call it what it is. You have to be good at office politics. Now, before you go and tell me that there are no politics in your company, I want you to think about the following:

- When there is a hiring freeze in the company, who is able to add head count?

- When budgets are frozen, who manages to secure new computers for her team?
- Who manages to land the best office space for his people when the company moves to a new location?

Again, these people are not manipulating others in order to gain favor. They are using influence (and sometimes position) to move their desires forward. I suggest you do the same.

Being known as the person who can cut through red tape and get things done is a good thing. You can use this skill to your benefit when looking to hire a top performer away from someone else or when hiring in general. Tell stories about some of the projects you've been able to push through or some of the outcomes your team has achieved because they have complete support from you as well as the organization. Discuss with your team strategies for how you can work around some of the barriers that may be standing in the way of success. Remind them you are willing to use your clout on their behalf.

SHIFT Communications president Amy Lyons talked with me about the importance of trust as it relates to influence and leadership. "Influence starts from trust. My ability to influence is directly related to how much trust I have built as a leader. I can then use influence to get to an end result," Lyons says. She shared the following example with me: "Let's say I'm speaking to a manager and I want to move her into a different position. If she trusts me and the fact that I'm operating from a place of advocacy, she will listen to me."

Trust is also a huge factor when working with clients. Lyons works in the PR space, which is, these days, highly competitive both in terms of talent and customers. "Our clients have to trust that we will operate with authenticity," notes Lyons. "I'm a big believer in building trust with little moments. It's something that is established over time. On any given day, I'm trying to convince, reassure, support, encourage, and motivate. I do that every day in little ways."

Lyons learned the art of influencing from the best. She started her career in politics, where she had the opportunity to work with Massachusetts senator Ted Kennedy and Chuck Robb, at the time the junior senator from Virginia. "When you work in politics and with politicians," says Lyons, "you are surrounded by people whose focus is getting what they want. I got to see influence firsthand. I saw traits that I wanted to mirror." Lyons learned quickly that being audience centric was key. Her belief that you need to understand the person you are talking to is something she has carried with her in her role as a leader at SHIFT Communications and when she interfaces with clients.

When you think about it, everything you do as a leader requires the use of influence. You may be trying to get an employee to embrace a new assignment or asking the boss for additional resources for your team. You may be trying to win a new contract or getting a current client to renew. Most likely, you are influencing people every day, even if you don't realize you are doing so. The question is, how effective are you at influencing, and would improving in this area help you to better attract employees, customers, and profits? The answer to the latter part of the question for most of us is yes!

Persuasion Self-Test: How Convincing Are You?

Use this tool to assess your persuasion abilities. Do your best to answer these questions honestly. This self-test will be most useful to you if you have honest results.

PERSUASION SELF-TEST: HOW CONVINCING ARE YOU? *Please rate yourself in each of the following areas:*	Ratings 4 = All the time 3 = Most of the time 2 = Sometimes 1 = Rarely 0 = Never N/A = Not applicable
1. I build trusting relationship before I try to persuade.	
2. I listen intently to others before using persuasion.	
3. When persuading, I share positive outcomes that came about as a result of others trusting me in the past.	
4. When persuading, I always demonstrate what's in it for the other person.	
5. I'm open to input from others and will adjust my thinking when appropriate.	

PERSUASION SELF-TEST: HOW CONVINCING ARE YOU? *Please rate yourself in each of the following areas:*	Ratings 4 = All the time 3 = Most of the time 2 = Sometimes 1 = Rarely 0 = Never N/A = Not applicable
6. When persuading, I clearly communicate the benefits of my ideas.	
7. I always consider my audience before putting together my persuasion strategy.	
8. I'm not afraid to retreat, should I realize that a request is no longer appropriate.	
9. I give before asking.	
10. I use my position for the betterment of my people.	
11. I focus on the similarities I have with those I'm trying to persuade.	
12. When someone resists my ideas, I try to learn why and adjust my communication accordingly.	
13. I choose my words carefully when persuading.	
14. I'm aware of the tone I'm using when persuading and adjust when necessary.	
15. I try to establish positive relationships with people and do so without an agenda.	
16. I try to see things from the perspective of others.	
17. I regularly take time out of my day or week to get to know people in the organization.	
18. I use positive speech and use win-win language when persuading.	
19. I use persuasion for the benefit of others rather than solely for my own benefit.	
20. I recognize when my persuasion tactics are too intense and adjust them accordingly.	

Any area with a score of 2 or less shows deficiencies. You'll need to work on improving in these areas so that you can more effectively move people toward your way of thinking.

We'll talk more about how you can increase your influence in a bit. First, let's take a deeper dive into the common traits of persuasive leaders (I use the terms *persuasion* and *influence* interchangeably), so you can assess where you currently fit in the leadership magnetism equation in terms of persuasion.

Common Traits of Persuasive Leaders

In my consulting practice, I've had the opportunity to work with some highly persuasive leaders as well as those who needed my help to dial up the persuasiveness level of their management style. Here are some common traits of persuasive leaders.

Belief in Oneself

The first sale is to yourself. You have to honestly believe that you are deserving of what you are asking for. If you don't, people will see right through you, and your efforts will fail. Or if you do succeed, you will lose the trust you built the moment someone recognizes that even you don't believe in what you are requesting. Here's what I mean: suppose you are trying to persuade someone to leave an employer she's been with for the past ten years. This individual is known around town as a superstar. You have to honestly believe you are worthy of someone of this caliber and that you'll be able to keep her challenged in her new role. If you don't think you deserve to have someone who is that talented working for you, or if you don't believe this move would be mutually beneficial, you may get her to say yes, but it's doubtful that she will remain by your side for years to come. She'll quickly realize that you've done a heck of a sales job on her and will be gone before it's time for her mid-year performance review.

Relentlessness

Persuasive people never give up, no matter how unfavorable the future might look. This goes back to their beliefs. They honestly believe in what they are doing and asking for. They feel they'd be remiss if they weren't able to convince others to join in their quest.

Veteran broadcast journalist Barbara Walters is a prime example of relentlessness. Her persistence helped her break through the TV glass ceiling more than once. She was the first woman on *Today* in 1962 and the first woman co-anchor on the evening news with Harry Reasoner in 1976. Over the years, she's managed to score such high-profile interviews as Egypt's president Anwar Sadat and Cuban leader Fidel Castro. And who could forget her 1999 talk with Monica Lewinsky, which drew a record 74 million viewers? One can only imagine how many other journalists were hoping to land that interview!

I can say without a doubt that I encounter the most relentless leaders in the tech industry. It's such a competitive field these days that you have to be relentless in order to compete with the next start-up that pops up in your space. Leaders in tech have to be magnificent influencers. After all, they are often selling an out-of-this-world idea to someone who has never left the planet. Those who do this successfully are able to live another day to tell their story.

Empathy

There are times when use of empathy can help to move someone to your side. An example of this would be a situation where you need one of your people to accept an assignment that will require relocation. It's only natural that, if the person is married and especially if he has kids, he might express concern for how this move will impact his family. Demonstrating empathy and offering to provide whatever support is needed to ease the transition will help move this person closer to saying yes to the assignment.

Those leaders who put themselves in the other person's shoes are most likely to successfully persuade someone. Ask yourself how you might feel in the same circumstances and what might help you change your mind. When doing so, remember that logic makes people think and emotion makes people act. Empathy is a strong emotion. When people feel you understand their point of view, their resistance will drop as quickly as your winnings at a craps table in a Las Vegas casino. Use this power wisely or risk diluting its potency.

Boldness

Persuasive leaders are bold. They make declarative statements and give little thought to what others might think. Others admire these people — probably because many secretly wish they could be more like them. My mentor Alan Weiss is a bold leader. He speaks confidently and says what many of us are thinking. This kind of magnetism has enabled him to build a community of consultants that spans the globe.

Bold leaders aren't afraid to push back on ideas, nor are they worried about being popular. They are masters at attracting a following and have no problem convincing others to join them on their journey. President Donald Trump is a prime example of a bold leader. Say what you will about the guy, his election rallies were always standing room only and he persuaded millions of Americans to join him in his calling to "Make America Great Again."

You can increase your boldness by following my DGAH Model—the abbreviation stands for Don't Give a Hoot! You do this by

- Telling other people what they need to hear and not necessarily what they want to hear
- Not worrying about things you can't control
- Taking the position that you'd rather be respected than loved
- Not overthinking things
- Taking a position because you honestly believe it's the right thing to do, rather than just trying to stir up drama

Those who have adopted my DGAH model have told me they feel like they've gone from driving a minivan to a Maserati. They are more nimble, are able to take the curves in their organization more easily, and are turning a lot more heads now that they've gone from ordinary to bold. In a nutshell, they've moved from exhaustion to exhilaration. And who could argue with that?

Techniques to Help You Influence Up, Down, and All Around

The other day, I was talking with some colleagues about the Post-it Syndrome and how it is running rampart in organizations. Now don't get me wrong, I love Post-its and couldn't imagine a full life without these sticky little pieces of paper floating around my desk and stuffed into my wallet. However, the thing about Post-its is that they eventually lose their stickiness and fall to the ground, which creates chaos, at least in my world. I find the same thing happens when leaders fail to maintain their ability to influence. They go from being extremely sticky and having lots of people adhering to them to having a team that easily peels off and can't wait to take the next flight out of the company departure lounge.

Everyone is pretty busy these days, and it's easy to forget the basic principles behind influencing. Here's a little virtual Post-it you can use to remind yourself of steps you can take to effectively influence and increase your adhesion:

1. **Deposit daily into your bank of trust.** Do something every day to build trust. This way, if you have to make a withdrawal (e.g., you inadvertently broke a promise, etc.), you won't bankrupt your relationship.

2. **Check your relationship score.** Before making a request, determine whether your relationship is strong enough for the other party to honor that request. If not, go back to step one.

3. **Make sure your request is specific.** Tell the person *exactly* what you'd like him to do.

4. **Think W.I.F.M. (What's In It For Me).** Put yourself in the other person's place and always ask yourself why someone would consider your request—W.I.F.M.—then make that reason part of your request.

Let's put this together. You'd like an employee to shift over to a new account. You have high levels of trust and your relationship score is off the charts. You are in a good position to make an influencing request. Let's give it a go:

> Jane, we've worked with one another for quite some time now and I've been by your side as you've learned this business. I'd like you to consider making a lateral move to a new account. By that I mean, you'll use the skills you've mastered on this account and become my right-hand person on the new account. This way you'll have the full cycle agency experience, which in turn will best position you for a future promotion.

As you can see, all four steps are embedded in this request. Given this is so, I'd say you have a very high chance that this person will say yes to your request.

Continue to work on building your influencing skills, and you will see that in no time you will dramatically increase your ability to influence up, down, and all around the organization (and at home as well!).

Now that you know how to move people to your side, let's discuss some sticky performance issues that may at times make you wonder if magnetic leadership is really for you. (Spoiler Alert: It is!)

Gravitational Pull Exercise #8

Take the Persuasion Self-Test. What areas have I convinced you need improvement? Make notes for what you are willing to commit to in order to build trust and increase your influencing skills.

Chapter 9
Sticky Performance Issues: How Magnetic Leaders Charge Through

Wouldn't it be great if your magnetism could act as a shield and prevent sticky performance issues from penetrating your reputation? Well, it can! That is, it can if you put on your armor and toughen up.

In my work, I coach a lot of CEOs, many of whom have the same dreams and fears as those who report to them. Like you, these CEOs really want their people to succeed and may even take it personally when one of their people fails. But here's the thing: Dreams are great, and everyone wants to believe in fairy-tale endings. Reality can be quite a different story.

I recall my experience working with a client who was in the role of CEO for the first time in his career. He really wanted to see the good in everyone and gave many of his people second chances—and sometimes even third and fourth chances. His attempt to save the "world" almost cost him his sanity as well as his job. We worked together for about a year, and at the end of our time he said he had grown more than he thought was possible. Here is one of the most critical things he learned: you can't want more for your people than they want for themselves. In other words, you can only do so much to help an employee step up her game or work through a personal problem. The employee has to do the lion's share of the work. He also learned that situations that are brewing will not go away on their own without intervention. More often than not, the situation worsens.

The following advice will help shield you from the damage that can occur when sticky performance issues are either left unattended or handled poorly. Be sure to revisit this chapter from time to time, as sticky performance issues seem to find their way into organizations more often than not.

Underwhelming Job Performance

If I had an apple for every time I've had discussions with leaders about the underperformance of their direct reports, I'd have an orchard! Remember that earlier in this book I talked about conflict avoidance seeming to be a trait that many leaders (and their people) have mastered? Well, it's also the core of continuing poor performance of your team members.

Think about it this way. How do employees know they are not meeting your expectations if you never tell them? I get that you may not want to hurt their feelings, but wouldn't you want to know if you were in the position of a poorly performing employee? I know I would!

Underwhelming job performance usually happens because of one or more of the following:

- **Unclear expectations.** The employee was never really told what was expected of him.
- **Little, if any, feedback.** Most of us are so accustomed to working under the "if you don't hear from me, things are fine" style of leadership that we automatically assume that's how things work everywhere. Granted, it's a poor assumption, but it's one that many of us make.
- **Wrong hire or promotion.** It happens. You hire or promote someone who turns out not to be right for the job. You figure that, in time, things will get better. They rarely do.
- **No direction.** You'll have to own this one. It's difficult for anyone to thrive when the leader continually fails to give her employees direction.

As you can see from this list, the only thing that might get corrected on its own is the scenario in which the person who should have never been hired or promoted quits his job. Of course, leaders—including those who are magnetic—pray this will happen sooner rather than later. In my experience, here is what happens instead.

Those who are meeting and exceeding expectations watch closely and wonder why underperformers are able to get away with not meeting expectations. Some of these people will quickly decide they don't need to work as hard as they are working and will begin to adopt the habits of the poor performers. Others will question the effectiveness of the leader they are reporting to. This disenchantment will lead employees to actively seek a more magnetic leader or, at a minimum, become very open to discussions with those who may reach out to them with a job opportunity. In both of these cases, your magnetism is quickly tarnished, which, in turn, dulls any chance you have of continuing to pull and retain talent.

Take action the moment you recognize that the employee you thought you hired isn't the one showing up every day (assuming they are actually showing up). When you talk with the underperforming employee, cite the specific behaviors you are observing and review the expectations of the position. If it's clear your heart is in it more than the employee's, do everyone a favor. Release this person so he is free to find love again elsewhere.

From Boss to Therapist

I'm often asked to present webinars or speak at conferences in front of high-level executives. One of my most popular topics, by far, is "Am I Your Boss or Your Therapist?" Here's my story regarding the day I realized that the title on my business card should have been therapist rather than director of human resources.

I hired a young woman I'll call Felicia to work as a secretary in my department (you may know these people as executive assistants, since I think the title of secretary went out with high-waisted jeans). In any case, to describe Felicia as a problem child would be an understatement. She reminded me a bit of Pig-Pen in Charles Schultz's Peanuts comic strip. But instead of attracting dirt, Felicia attracted problems. First, there were boyfriend problems, which may have been brought on by her drinking problem. Then there were the episodes of roommate blowups that would make today's *Real Housewives of New Jersey* look like a show Disney would air. Every now and again one of her three ex-husbands would show up in her life, which created even more drama. (Did I mention she was only twenty-six years old?)

I was like many of you. I gave her a second chance, a third chance, and many more, as I lost count. Instead of working on the projects needed to move the company (and my personal career) forward, I worked on Felicia. She was a full-time job and then some—there were also the evenings I spent worrying, as the idea of suicide was something she had no qualms about discussing. (You see where I'm going here?)

I thought I could save Felicia, and Lord knows I tried, time and time again. It took me a while (okay, more than a while) to realize that what Felicia really needed was professional help. She finally started seeing a therapist, and I had to make the tough decision to end our relationship. She left the company and most likely found another leader like me who was, shall we say, a little too understanding.

Don't be like me. Everyone has problems—and some have more than others. I'm all for granting an employee time off to deal with a crisis that emerged as a result of a divorce, family illness, or other life event. But think twice if you have people lying on the couch in your office sharing their woes while you are left to work late into the evening so you can do the job you were hired to do.

When an employee brings her personal problems to the office and they affect her work or the work of those around her, you need to know right then and there that your only job is to refer her to a resource that can assist her. Start by checking to see if your company has an EAP (Employee Assistance Program). These programs are designed to identify and assist employees in resolving personal problems (e.g., financial stresses, family issues, emotional problems, substance/alcohol abuse) that may be adversely affecting the employee's performance. If only EAPs had been around when Felicia was in my care!

As a leader, your job is to make a troubled employee aware of resources such as the EAP. Your job is not to be like me and act as her mental health-care provider. You can also suggest the employee speak with a social worker from a nonprofit that specializes in problems like the one she is experiencing, or, if appropriate, a member of the clergy or a rabbi. Lots of options are available these days for those in need of help. Again, just make sure you don't cross the line from leader to full-time mental health provider or you'll end up like

I did—on someone else's couch trying to work through all the stress in my work life!

Conflict in the Workplace

Here's the thing about conflict. It can come out of nowhere. You may be able to relate to the following common scenario: things appear to be fine in your organization. There is a sense of calm flowing above the cubicles. Employees are interacting in a respectful way and are working well as a team. Then your company lands a huge new contract. Everyone is working overtime. Voices are rising and fingers are pointing. The majority of your day is spent playing referee. You walk outside to see if there is a full moon in sight. When you return, there is another employee in your office waiting to complain about a coworker.

Conflict in the workplace is inevitable. When you throw a group of people together in close quarters and put them under some pressure, differences are bound to surface. But the news is not all bad. Some conflict in the organization can be beneficial. Differences of opinion encourage creativity and progress. If addressed early, conflict can also provide insight into larger issues that may be brewing. However, more often than not, employee conflict is left unresolved. When this happens, the boss is seen as someone who is unable to keep peace and harmony in her workgroup. Employees pick up on this stress and may choose to seek greener (and calmer) pastures. If you want to retain your reputation as a leader who has a cohesive team, then you'll need to learn how to deal with conflict.

Learning how to handle conflict effectively can actually help you prevent conflict from happening in the first place. Follow along with me and you'll see why this is so. Ask yourself the following questions.

Was I Clear in My Communication?

Conflict in the workplace can occur when a leader is vague, for example, when he doesn't specify what he expects or who will ultimately be responsible for the task assigned. Be clear when communicating with team members and don't be afraid to ask people if they understand exactly what you are asking.

Is There One Person on My Team Who Seems to Be "Captain Conflict"?

This is the person who is always leading the charge . . . in the opposite direction. By now you may have come to the conclusion that this person is doing more to harm the team than good. Consider a new play and tell Captain Conflict he's just been given free agent status!

Are There Enough Resources to Go Around?

Conflict often arises when there are not enough resources to go around. When this happens, people immediately shift into a scarcity mindset. They become like kids who are given one piece of chocolate and told to share it with a sibling. All hell breaks lose! Are you asking the impossible? Are you expecting people on your team to get their jobs done without adequate resources? If conflicts are arising, it may be time to reevaluate what you are asking or, at a minimum, to advocate for additional resources so that people don't hunker down into scarcity mode.

Are You Secretly Hoping the Conflict Will Go Away on Its Own?

I'm sorry, but hope is not a strategy. Conflict doesn't normally go away on its own. In fact, it usually gets worse when left unattended. Just ask someone who has a disagreement with his spouse before leaving for work. He may attempt to go home and forget anything ever happened. Of course his partner will quickly remind him that everything is *not* fine! Address conflict head on the moment it arises. Do this if you really want to restore peace and harmony—both at work and at home.

Taking On Someone's Problem Employee

Marla Kaplowitz, CEO of global advertising agency MEC North America, knows all too well about inheriting a problem employee from someone else. "I inherited a problem employee who was very difficult," notes Kaplowitz. "The employee had mental challenges. She had a temper tantrum one night in the office and started throwing things. We probably should have done something right then and there. Things got worse.

Right as we were about to put her on probation, she went out on short-term disability." Understandably, this person's direct manager felt threatened and asked Kaplowitz to step in and manage this employee.

Kaplowitz learned a lot from this experience, including the need to always seek additional references before hiring someone. Don't rely on the references the person hands you. Locating additional references is easier to do these days because you can go onto sites like LinkedIn to see if the candidate is connected to someone you know as well. Always call references, even if a candidate has been referred to you. As I discussed in the section on workplace conflict, address a problem head on the moment it becomes clear that you and the employee are not going to live happily ever after together.

I've seen managers move problem employees around the organization as if they were tires being rotated on a car. Eventually, the tread wears thin and performance is affected. The same thing happens with a problem employee. Let's all take a vow and promise one another that we won't do to others what we don't want done to us! We'll deal with our problem employees, even if that means we have to be the ones to tell them that we won't be driving off into the sunset together.

Sex in the Workplace and Office Romance

Ah, love is grand—until it happens on your watch or, as *Vanity Fair* would like you to believe, under your desk. A number of years ago, I was invited to be on *The O'Reilly Factor* to discuss sex in the workplace with Bill O'Reilly. *Vanity Fair* had just published an article claiming that office romance was alive and well in workplaces and that employees were having sex with one another at work during and after business hours. I pushed back on O'Reilly (no pun intended), and told him I thought the survey results were ridiculous. Having worked in HR for a number of years and being very involved in the HR community, I had never encountered a situation where employees were having sex *in* the workplace, nor had any of my colleagues shared stories like this with me. It was a good move on my part, as he went after the woman from *Vogue*, who was also a guest, and I left the show unscathed!

Given how much time employees spend at the office these days, it's not uncommon for sparks to fly at work and for coworkers to date. According to CareerBuilder's 2015 annual office romance survey, dating a coworker is a fairly common occurrence, with 37 percent of workers saying they have dated a coworker at least once during their career.[1]

You need to be prepared to handle workplace romance situations, as they may well occur in your department or organization. First and foremost, know the rules. In some organizations it's okay to date someone who works for the same company (as long as there is no direct reporting relationship), and in others, this is frowned upon. Some companies have employees sign "Love Contracts," in which both parties acknowledge they are entering into a relationship of their own free will. This move helps to protect the company from legal action, should either of the two parties decide it's time to go to court.

Personality Disorders

As Kaplowitz points out, sometimes employees who are behaving erratically have personality disorders. Unless you are a licensed social worker or have an MD after your name, don't attempt to use rational tactics to deal with irrational behavior. Instead, refer the employee to your company Employee Assistance Program (EAP) or encourage him to seek professional help. When doing so, focus on observed behavior. For example, having a fit in the office in front of you and the team is not what most would consider normal behavior. Point out how this behavior is impacting the employee's reputation, and let him know you are coming from a place of concern.

Hopefully, you won't encounter an employee who has a mental illness that is extreme. If you do, trust your instincts. Workplace violence is real. The Bureau of Labor Statistics' Census of Fatal Occupational Injuries (CFOI) reported 14,770 workplace homicide victims between 1992 and 2012.[2] If an employee makes a threat, take the threat seriously. Report the incident to the police and follow their guidance.

Unethical Behavior

We've all heard about the shenanigans that go on in organizations, and some of these border on unethical behavior. Many situations certainly cross the line. When it's happening on your watch, you have no choice but to investigate before an employee's shady reputation becomes part of your legacy.

I tell my advisory clients to assume good intent. We all have different values. I may believe something is ethical when you don't and vice versa. Have a private conversation with the employee in question so you can better understand his thinking. If the behavior involves a clear ethical violation, such as selling company secrets to a competitor, then you know what you need to do. Fire this guy.

If the situation is not as severe and it appears to be a minor infraction, you can decide the best course of action. This may include anything from a verbal warning to probation.

It's important to understand that, from time to time, every leader faces employee problems. If it seems to be happening to you more often than it happens to your colleagues in leadership positions, then the problem may very well be you—something worth considering. Now that you've got some strategies to manage through some tough situations, let's move on to what some people are calling Armageddon—the mass exodus of employees from organizations.

Gravitational Pull Exercise #9

Make a list of the problems you've been avoiding with your employees. Vow to tackle these situations head on. Do it now.

Notes

1. CareerBuilder, "Workers Name Their Top Office Romance Deal Breakers in New CareerBuilder Survey," February 11, 2015, http://www.careerbuilder.com/share/aboutus/pressreleasesdetail.aspx?sd=2%2F11%2F2015&id=pr868&ed=12%2F31%2F2015.
2. Bureau of Labor Statistics, "Census of Fatal Occupational Injuries (CFOI)," http://www.cdc.gov/niosh/topics/violence/.

Chapter 10
Getting Great Employees to Stick Around

Recently, I was the keynote speaker at the Boston Evanta CHRO (Chief Human Resource Officer) Leadership Conference, where I had a dynamic conversation with global HR leaders on "How to Create a Solar System of Talent." One of the CHROs told me that he thought employees were receiving monthly calls from headhunters regarding new opportunities. I suggested that the people in his organization were receiving calls daily! I then asked the leaders in the room to raise their hands if a headhunter had called them about a new opportunity within the last week. *More than 75 percent* of the people in the room raised their hands! That's just crazy. Let's face it. It's going to take a lot more than a prayer and some free beer on Fridays to hang onto your talent.

That got me thinking. What's the point of hiring great people if you can't keep them? You may as well go after mediocre people, as they are a heck of a lot easier to secure. Of course, if you followed this strategy you'd have to kiss your clients and profits goodbye, as most would scatter like pollen on a spring day.

We all know of companies that have a reputation for churning employees. They woo top talent with promises of big signing bonuses, fat paychecks, and fancy offices that overlook the water. They throw in what appear to be some awesome benefits, such as on-site dry cleaning services and meals to go for those who are too exhausted to cook after work. It all sounds great until the employee wakes up and realizes she's just sold her soul to the devil. She quickly finds there is no such thing as a free lunch (or in this case, a free dinner) and she is required to work twelve-hour days. Some such employees will remain in their roles because they are really in it just for the money, while others will do a deep dive off the company roof deck the moment a better (and more sane) offer arrives on the horizon.

This insanity of offering more perks and creating workspaces that resemble a McDonald's playground more than an office has got to stop. It doesn't work as a retention strategy. Even kids quickly tire of and outgrow play spaces. Here's what you should be doing instead.

The Leaving Speech

Magnetic leader Rob Nixon, CEO of PANALITIX, wrote a Facebook post one day that took my breath away. I asked him if I could share it with others and he readily agreed. Keep in mind that Nixon was a guy who used to lose great people on a regular basis. Not any more. He took a hard look inside himself and became very clear about what he wanted his legacy to be and what he wanted his employees to experience. Here's his post, what he calls "The Leaving Speech."

> Today marks the end of a five-years-and-two-months era. But it's also the start of a new one. One of our star performers, Sharon McClafferty, is leaving to look for new opportunities. She started as a sales coordinator and was quickly promoted into the role of sales where she quickly started outselling seasoned professionals. Within twelve months she was the sales manager, where she grew and led a team of seven people. She had never sold anything before joining our company, yet in five years she has sold in excess of $5 million of new revenue. An absolute superstar. When Sharon sells, she doesn't sell. That's the difference. She is an amazing relationship builder who makes a difference to those that she engages. She tells me she has done over 750 consultations to accountants, which is awesome.

> On or close to the day she started, I had the "leaving speech" with her. It went something like this:

> "Sharon, welcome to the team. We're thrilled you're here. I am sure you're the right person for the job and I know there is a lot going on this week. I just wanted to talk to you for a few minutes about the day you leave. You will leave one day; everyone does. I know this is your first day but I know you'll leave sometime in the future, so I figured we should talk about it now. I have a number of hopes and desires for that inevitable day. Firstly, I hope we part on good company. I don't want someone to fire you because you didn't work

out or make you redundant because of a business downturn. Secondly, I hope that you learn a lot, contribute a lot, and have a lot of fun. Thirdly, I hope that you live by our values, service, and culture standards, and the standards we set become part of your life. And lastly, when you look back at this block of time, no matter how long it is, you look back on it fondly as an amazing part of your career. Welcome to the team. That's all I wanted to say."

I do this with every new team member close to the day they start. Sharon has ticked all those boxes and she has grown into an extraordinary professional.

I tell all my clients to compose their own leaving speech, and I suggest you do the same. Here are some questions to get you started:

- What hopes and dreams do you have for your people?
- How will they be better off having known you?
- What would you like them to say about their experience working for you, as well as the company?

Now imagine being a new employee on the other side of the desk and hearing Nixon's speech. If you're like me, you are probably thinking you're *finally* working for someone who is deeply concerned about what you experience under his direction. Believe me when I tell you that it doesn't get much better than that. I doubt many people will voluntarily leave a leader who is deeply committed to making sure their last day is as fulfilling as their first day, and that every day in between is just as meaningful.

What Today's Workers Expect from Their Leaders

You'd think that with all the technology available, employers would know exactly what workers are really seeking from their leaders. I believe many already know what I'm about to tell you. But here's the thing. It's a lot easier to provide free snacks or buy a Ping-Pong table for the office than it is to provide the things I'm about to suggest.

If you believe, like I do, that money doesn't buy happiness or employee loyalty, then read on.

Respect

When I coach executives, I usually interview members of their team to gain a better understanding of how these employees view their leader. It's not uncommon for someone to tell me her boss frequently speaks to her in a disrespectful manner or that he has no respect for employees' time. How difficult can it really be to treat people the way you'd like to be treated? Think about this the next time you are about to address an employee in a way you'd probably find offensive and reframe what you are about to say. Employees who feel respected by their leaders are more likely to stick with the company than those who don't. And remember, these days no one has to stay in a relationship that isn't based on mutual respect.

Community and Purpose

Employees today want to know how the work they are doing will ultimately make the world a better place. This is a far cry from when I first started in the workplace. Back then we had two purposes: make money and score a corner office. Having achieved the latter, at the ripe old age of twenty-four years old, I can tell you it was all downhill from there. No matter how much money I made, it was never enough. Eventually, I found my purpose, back before having a purpose was cool. So for those of you who are still trying to figure out the purpose of your organization, I suggest you begin by thinking about the following: If your company went away tomorrow, would anyone care? If your answer is, "Yes! Millions of people would die if we weren't on this planet developing life-saving drugs," then your purpose is clear. The rest of you may have a little more work to do, but I promise you, your purpose is there.

As a leader, it's your job to create a culture that is purpose driven and focused on the customer. You also need to help employees understand how their work impacts the organization's ability to achieve its goals as well as profits. People who work in a healthy culture and are committed to a cause have no problem getting up every day and coming to work. They do so with a level of passion that cannot be had with more perks or stock options that may very well be underwater as soon as the next tech bubble bursts. You can do this in a number of ways, including bringing your customers in to your office to talk about how much better their business or their life is because of the work that your people are doing. Or if that's not possible, you can take your employees out into the field the next time you have a meeting with a client so they gain a direct line of sight to the people they are working to help. You can also ask your clients how they are better off as a result of doing business with you. Spread the word around the organization by e-mailing client responses to employees. Post these responses on company bulletin boards and intranets so that you can keep customer successes front and center.

Interesting Work Assignments

Imagine that you didn't have to leave your employer in order to take on more interesting work. Many people dream of this, but have a very different reality. Their employers go outside the company to hire rather than giving internal people an opportunity to take on a new challenge. This scenario reminds me of the shiny penny syndrome, in which everyone is looking for the next great thing to come along. What if that next great thing is right in your organization?

Some of my clients have job rotation programs that provide employees with opportunities to work in different environments and on different projects without leaving the organization. You don't have to be part of a huge business to make this happen. What you do need are bright people who adapt well to change. Before going outside to fill a new role, take a look at the people inside your organization and be open to employees contributing in a different way. For example, if you have someone in your organization who is doing a great job at recruiting (which is basically sales), consider giving him an opportunity to work on the sales team. Make it okay for him to give it a go by letting him know that if he doesn't enjoy the work, he can go back to his old job. In the meantime, you can backfill that job with a contract recruiter.

Another way to keep work interesting is to give employees an opportunity to take on some of your responsibility. This will free you up to do more stimulating work, as well.

Career Development and Growth

The other day, I was sitting at dinner with the heads of HR from Staples and Bose and the newly retired CHRO from Analog Devices. I asked them what they thought today's employees wanted most from their employers. One of them blurted out, "Career development," and everyone else nodded in agreement. They then went on to tell me that employees who haven't been in their jobs all that long are asking questions like, "What are you going to do to help me prepare for my next career move? What kind of training are you willing to give me? How do I get a mentor? When can I have a coach? When do I get promoted?"—this last question is often asked several months on the job!

Employees at all levels of the organization are seeking to improve their skills and take on more interesting work. Companies like my client General Motors are investing heavily in career development offerings for their employees across the globe, at all stages of their careers. GM prides itself on being an innovative organization, and the company recently announced a joint venture with Lyft to begin testing self-driving taxies. This level of innovation requires talent that is always pushing the boundaries of what we think is humanly possible (although in this case there will be no humans). Innovation this level requires a company-wide commitment to a continuous investment in the people side of the business.

I understand that not all of you have the resources that a Fortune 500 company has. There are plenty of options for you as well. Coaching, group coaching, job rotations, on-site training, and reimbursement for conferences are all options that won't break the bank. I caution you not to base your investment decision solely on price. While a one-day off-site training program for $99 may seem like a great deal, you simply don't know what you are getting. And you can spend thousands of dollars to send your employee to an off-site training program and still not know what you're getting.

For example, last month I was in Los Angeles attending a consulting conference and I came upon an employee who was registering people for an American Management Association (AMA) course. She looked bored as can be. I smiled as I walked by but was unable to break her cold stare.

I then tried to engage her in conversation and asked her the name of the session. She replied in a low, apathetic voice, "Emotional intelligence." I doubt she saw the puzzled look on my face, as she hadn't bothered to look me in the eye when she mumbled those words.

For those of you who aren't familiar with the term emotional intelligence, the *Oxford Dictionary* defines emotional intelligence as, "a person's capacity to be aware of, control and express one's emotions, and to handle interpersonal relationships judiciously and empathetically." I left thinking that if the AMA couldn't hire someone with emotional intelligence to represent its program on emotional intelligence, what could the program possibly offer? I'll let you draw your own conclusion.

If you are serious about developing and keeping your good people, ask people in your network for referrals to developmental opportunities they have found to be of value or for the name of a consultant who can help you boost the performance and level of commitment for the employees you wish to retain. When you think about how much it costs each time a valuable employee leaves your firm, you'll soon realize that this nominal investment will more than pay for itself.

Clear Expectations and Meaningful Feedback

Oh, brother. This just in: according to the Harris Poll Interact Survey, 69 percent of managers dislike communicating with staff.[1] They are especially uncomfortable offering criticism that might cause employees to flare up. As a result, many simply don't provide difficult feedback. If this describes you, I'm going to suggest you either get more comfortable giving people honest feedback or consider moving into a role that doesn't require managing the work of others.

Let's assume you are reading this book because you are looking for advice on how to improve your leadership skills. Here's how you can dramatically improve in providing clear expectations and meaningful feedback.

- **Be kind and be direct.** Being direct does not require being harsh. In fact, beating around the bush actually feels like torture for the person receiving the feedback. When giving feedback, be brief and support your statements with examples of behavior to illustrate your point.

- **Listen.** Listening provides a space in which people feel heard and respected. A momentary pause enables both parties to process what is being said and allows them to move forward together to make a positive change.
- **Don't take reactions personally.** It's easy to get emotional when you are having what is, for many, an unpleasant conversation. Acknowledge the emotions both parties are feeling, which will help decrease the stress levels felt by you and the person you are speaking with.
- **Show up and don't rush off.** Yikes! No one likes tough conversations. Don't make it worse by showing up, dumping all the negative thoughts you've been bottling up, and departing like a hit-and-run driver. Slow down and allow time for a meaningful two-way dialogue to take place.

Leaders who learn how to provide clear expectations and honest feedback are able to create a culture of connection that defies the laws of gravity. Try it and let me know what transpires.

Authenticity and Transparency

I asked Wendy Foster, president and CEO of Big Brothers, Big Sisters of Massachusetts Bay and also a client of mine, what she believes employees want most from their leaders, and she told me, "Our work with you has amplified some of the things that I'm thinking about. People want their leaders to be authentic. They want to be able to trust their leaders and know they have the best needs of the employees and organization in mind. They also want clarity on the direction and vision and help understanding where they fit into all of this." She went on to say, "People want to have meaning and purpose. There is something bigger than a business metric or profit margin."

I first met Foster when a satisfied client suggested that she work with me. Her transparency from the get-go was notable, as was her spark. I knew right away that working with her would be an incredible experience, and I was not wrong. There were times when I had to deliver news that others would have felt defensive about. Not Foster. She took the information in and said, "We have an opportunity to do better." She openly communicated the results I uncovered to her people, and she made it a point to do this in person rather than hide behind e-mail. I couldn't be more pleased with the outcomes she and her team are achieving in terms of employee attraction and retention. She tells me she couldn't have done it without me. But if the truth were known, we never could have moved the organization forward as quickly as we have if she had not been open and transparent with me and with the people she serves.

The next time you ask yourself how much information you should share with others and what you should shield them from, I'd encourage you to think of Foster. If you are a good leader and you have surrounded your-self with a solid team, then you should have no worries telling people the whole truth. Of course, if you have people working in jobs where perhaps they shouldn't be and you don't have a trusting relationship—that's a completely different situation.

Equitable Pay

Some people believe money doesn't matter. Those are usually the people who have enough money and then some. The cost of living is astronomical in many cities, and some companies are not moving their pay structures fast enough to keep up with what people need to make in order to survive. You can't blame someone who is barely scraping by if she leaves for a $20,000 raise. But here's the thing. Many of these people really don't want to leave you, and they won't if you can find a way for them to stay.

Young people today are coming out of college with record levels of debt. I'm not asking you to play a violin for them, since many could have attended a lesser-known school and graduated with far less debt. (Then again, would you have considered hiring them if they didn't attend one of the higher-ranked schools?) We can all agree that at some point it no longer matters where you attended school. Of course, when we have that aha moment, we're usually mid-way into paying off our student loans. We look around and see that many of our friends are no longer living in their parents' basements. They have moved out and moved on. We begin to question what will it take for us to do the same, and usually the only solution we can see is to take a new job for more money.

Here's what I've found in my work with hundreds of businesses: equal isn't fair. Here's what I mean by this. You have two people with the same job title entering a position with different levels of experience yet similar pay. The two employees make comparable pay, but one of them is contributing significantly more than the other. How can this be fair? It's not. I'm not going to place all the blame on the manager, as, more often than not, the compensation policies are out of whack. Case in point, one of my clients only allowed promotions twice a year, and employees had to have six months under their belts before they could be considered for promotion. So let's say the promotion dates were July 1 and January 1. If an employee was hired on December 1 and was a decent employee, he could be promoted (and usually was) to the next level in July, and this brought with it a bump in pay. An employee hired on January 2 would need to wait almost a full year for a promotion and more money, even if he did an outstanding job.

When it comes to compensation, there is no perfect system, but as a leader you should always be looking at the status quo and making recommendations where appropriate. Do this often, as what seemed fair only a year ago may no longer be equitable.

Five Things Employees Don't Need from Their Bosses

No conversation about employee retention would be complete without a discussion of what employees don't need from their bosses. Here are five of those things. You may think of others.

1. **Friendship.** Employees need a boss, not a friend. Go on anyone's Facebook page and you'll see that most people have more friends than they know what to do with. Here's what they do need. They

need a boss who will give them direction, provide feedback, and help them grow into their full potential.

2. **Parenting.** If you've got an employee who is considerably younger (and who doesn't these days), you may be tempted to offer parental advice. Do not do this, even if asked. This person is your employee; and if this is employee is not your son or daughter, then you are not the parent.

3. **More work.** Everyone seems to be overloaded these days, and the last thing employees need from their boss is more work. Pouring more work on someone who already has a full load demonstrates that you don't respect her time. Do yourself and the employee a favor; hire a temp, bring in an intern, or add a person to your head count. Otherwise, you may soon find that you have that employee's job to do as well as your own.

4. **Favoritism.** Remember when you thought Mom liked your sibling more than you? It hurt and didn't exactly make you feel like pitching in with your sister or brother to do whatever was asked. The same thing happens at work. If employees feel you are showing favoritism to another employee, they'll quickly take note and will do little to assist that person. So much for teamwork, eh?

5. **Hearing about your problems.** The last thing your people need is to hear about your so-called terrible life. They have their own worries. Confide in a friend or a therapist, not in your employees.

As you can see, the leader is the one who really has *the* most impact on the employee and customer experience. What you do with this power will determine whether the line outside your door is filled with people who want to work for you or whether it's made up of those who can't wait to board the next flight out.

The last thing I want to mention in this chapter is a question I'm often asked: *Can I have too much stickiness?* My response is, "You betcha!" Not everyone you meet is a keeper. In the next chapter we'll discuss how to release employees who are unable to release themselves.

> **Gravitational Pull Exercise #10**
>
> Write the leaving speech you will deliver to your employees in their first week of employment. Feel free to send it to me at Roberta@ matusonconsulting.com for a critique.

Note

1. Interact, "New Interact Report: Many Leaders Shrink from Straight Talk with Employees," Harris Poll, February 2015, http://www.interactauthentically.com/ new-interact-report-many-leaders-shrink-from-straight-talk-with-employees/.

Chapter 11
Unstuck: Releasing Employees Who Cannot Release Themselves

I'll admit that I didn't appreciate being laid off when it happened to me, but now I fully comprehend the importance of cutting off the dead branches of an organization in order to make the rest of the company viable. I call this corporate pruning. If you prune on a regular basis, getting rid of employees who are dying on the vine, you'll most likely be able to avoid the terrible and often deadly reductions in force that we so often read about or personally experience.

Early in my career, I was "riffed"—corporate lingo for being let go so that the company can save money. Being young and confused, I asked my coworker why I was chosen. He was more senior than I was, and he told me that he was being kept on because he could do my job and his. Fair enough, as I knew he was right. But that didn't make it any easier for me to digest. If the company had regularly rid the workplace of underperformers, we might not have been in the situation where cuts were needed. But what did I know? I was only twenty-three years old at the time.

Years later, I've come up with what I call the Rosebud Leadership Principle. If you've ever tended rosebushes, you know that in order for the bush to flourish and produce beautiful blooms, it needs to be cut back on a regular basis. The same thing must happen in order for businesses to flourish. Often the people you hire when you are starting your business are not the people who will be able to take your business to the next level. This means that you may have to trim your workforce from time to time, in order to promote new growth. I'm a perfect case in point. I always tell people that if I had come over on the *Mayflower*, I would have certainly been a key player in setting up the colony. However, you would not have wanted me hanging around, as I'm all about strategy and process. You'd want me moving on to the next patch of land and getting that ready to colonize. I was like that in the corporate world. I'd go into organizations and set up their HR departments from scratch. When that was over and we went into maintenance mode, I'd grow bored and would move on to something else.

I believe it's important for leaders to assess their talent on a regular basis. I call this rebalancing the talent portfolio. Perhaps you have too many risk takers in your organization, and they are not serving you well now that you are in maintenance mode. Or you made some bad picks that you've been hanging onto for way too long. Just as a financial advisor helps clients keep their stock portfolio balanced, I help my clients ensure that their talent pool can thrive in both a bear and a bull market. And no matter what our intentions were going in, we usually wind up having to transition people out of the organization. I'm going to share with you how we do this in a way that has people thanking us on their way out the door. But first let's discuss when it's time to cut ties.

Seven Signs It's Time to Let Go

I've been in this business long enough to know that there are clear signs it's time to cut ties with employees. Here are seven of them.

1. **You want things to work out more than your employee does.** Have you ever tried to push a string? It's very difficult to do and the string usually winds up in a tangled mess. The same thing happens when you are more invested in helping an employee work things out than he is. Simply stated, it doesn't work.
2. **Drama, drama, drama.** Every day it's something else. Wherever this person goes, drama follows. Quite frankly it's exhausting. You've gone from a place of business to a workplace that closely resembles a telenovela. It's time to yell, "Cut!"
3. **He's just not that into you.** The employee has lost interest. Understand that there will be little you can do to make him like you again. Let him go so he can find true love elsewhere.
4. **Mismatched skills.** You need a rainmaker and what you have is someone who can barely make it drizzle. There are some traits, such as assertiveness and enthusiasm, that simply cannot be taught. Best to part ways so you can find a better match.
5. **Time's up!** You don't have the time or resources to bring this person up to speed. Every day that you spend trying is another day taken

away from someone or something else. Setting this person free is a gift to you both. You are freed up to help the rest of the team move forward, and the underperforming employee can now find a job for which she is better suited.

6. **You're changing. He's not.** Some people have more difficulty with change than others. If the company is going through a shift, as companies often do, and an employee is resistant to change, then you must release that person, as he will never be happy in an environment where change is the only constant.

7. **You've outgrown each other.** It happens. People outgrow one another. You may have an employee who was the right fit when you were a small, emerging tech business. You're now a mature company and this person prefers the daily buzz associated with a start-up. Shake hands and say goodbye before you begin to resent each other.

Timeless Tips on Thoughtful Terminations

Regardless of how careful you are in terms of hiring, eventually you will hire or promote someone who doesn't turn out to be what you had hoped for. Knowing someone's time is up is one thing. Actually letting a person go is another. Employee terminations are never easy. If the day does comes when it *is* easy, I'm going to suggest you look for another line of work. That said, let's talk about what many of you may be wondering. Is it really possible to thoughtfully terminate someone? The answer is yes! Here's what that I tell my advisory clients when they must say goodbye to an employee.

Speed Matters

I received an S.O.S. call from a friend of mine who owns a travel agency. He was sending out a distress signal because he had to terminate one of his people. He started the conversation by saying, "I probably should have done this sixteen years ago." Take action the moment you realize an employee is no longer the right person for the job. For some companies, that may mean putting someone on a performance planner. For others, that may mean releasing them right away. Once you make the decision that the manager is no longer suitable, take action, as things will likely not get better. They will only get worse.

Show R.E.S.P.E.C.T.

Aretha Franklin sang about it back in 1967 and it still rings true. I've seen too many frustrated leaders treat those they are about to terminate as if they are radioactive waste. Their hands-off approach leads to ill will all around, not to mention lawsuits. You liked this person well enough to hire him, so demonstrate respect as you transition him out of the company.

Be Clear

I've heard stories of people asking for raises at the same time their employers were discussing their poor performance and their impending termination. Do yourself and the employee a favor. Be very clear that the conversation you are about to embark on is the *end* of the road rather than the beginning of a new path toward a wonderful future together.

Be Honest

Telling someone how great she is and then terminating her during the same meeting never ends well. Be honest and succinct. The termination conversation isn't the time to coach someone on what she could have done differently to have kept her job, nor is it the time to tell her how great she is. This will only confuse the employee and may result in legal action. The next time you are tempted to try to soften the blow, picture yourself giving a deposition and saying, "Yes, I told her she was a pretty good leader and I then followed that statement with all the reasons she wasn't meeting my expectations in terms of her team." That image alone should be enough to convince you not to make this all-too-common mistake.

Make It a Win–Win

I've heard many stories where it was quite clear that the person doing the firing was going into the conversation looking to win the battle. The boss left the meeting feeling victorious, when in fact he was anything but.

A true win happens when the person you are firing extends his hand to thank you. I've had this happen to me a number of times. Why would an employee who was being fired do this? Because whenever possible, I looked for ways to help the person exit with his ego intact, which created a win-win and increased my magnetism.

Keep It Short and Sweet

A termination meeting is one of those times in life where brevity is key. There is no reason to rehash what's already been said. (You have had conversations about those areas where the employee hasn't been meeting your expectations, right?) There's no point in dragging the employee back through all her failures and why you are so terribly disappointed in her performance. Most likely, she is a heck of a lot more disappointed in the way things have worked out than you are. After all, you're still employed and she is about to go home and tell a loved one she's just been canned.

Cite the reason for the termination and, if need be, provide several examples that support why you will be parting ways. Don't attempt to soften the blow by telling the employee you are laying her off, when in fact you are terminating her for lack of performance. You don't want to set up an expectation that you may call the employee back to work, when it would have to snow in Cuba before you'd consider rehiring this person!

Remember That Environment Matters

Conducting a sensitive conversation in an open office environment can be challenging, because sound travels when you are in a sea of cubicles. Be sure to reserve a quiet private space so that you can have a candid conversation.

Timing matters as well. Terminating an employee during peak business hours is probably not the best in terms of timing. I suggest that you hold these conversations toward the end of the workday, as that will permit the employee to exit without having to do what I call the perp walk. That's when a person is escorted out of the office with belongings in hand, for all to see.

Prepare, Practice, and Release

A termination conversation is not one of those situations where you want to go in there and wing it. Take it from me. The more disorganized you are, the more painful the conversation will be. Take some time to compose your thoughts. You'll also want to make sure you have everything you need at hand (e.g., final paycheck, unemployment insurance information, health insurance continuation information, etc.) before entering the room to begin this conversation. The last thing you want is for the employee to be sitting in your office longer than he needs to while you scramble around trying to run down payroll so you can get a final check issued.

Practice what you are going to say so you aren't stumbling over your words. Then do the humane thing. Bring the employee into your office and quickly release him. Give the employee time to process what's been said and to ask questions before offering to escort him out of your office.

Let the Employee Guide Your Farewell

What do you say when all is done? A simple handshake and a thank you (when appropriate) may be all that is needed. But for this part, you'll need to follow the other person's lead. Some employees will want you to go back over every detail that has occurred since the day they started. You'll have to politely decline. Others will want to get out of your office faster than you'll want them to depart. Let them do so. When they leave the office, be sure to gather your team to let them know a team member will not be returning. When pressed for more information (and you will be pressed), respectfully decline to give it.

Mistakes to Avoid at All Costs

Here are some common mistakes you want to avoid when it comes to terminating employees.

Blaming Others

Here's my favorite line: "Corporate says we have to let you go." Really? Who the heck is corporate? Strong leaders take responsibility for their actions. If you are the one letting someone go, own it.

Choosing Inappropriate Language

"We need to let you go so we can bring in people with fresh ideas." I've heard this line more times than I can remember. It's code for, "We are getting rid of you because you are old and we are going to replace you with young people." Watch your language. The words you choose could easily be the end of you as well.

Letting Someone Else Do the Deed

In the movie *Up in the Air* George Clooney is a hired hand who travels around the country firing people. Sometimes reality mirrors fiction. The husband of a friend of mine starred in the role of victim during a similar scene; someone from corporate swooped into his office and fired him without warning. The person left as quickly as he arrived, leaving my friend's husband in a state of disarray. No matter what happens, don't allow someone else to do your dirty work. Every employee deserves a respectable exit. Your job is to make it so.

Lacking Compassion

I'm sorry that you are in the uncomfortable situation of having to tell someone he is about to lose his job. Yet your focus should be on the person who is about to get the news and his situation. When it comes to showing compassion during employee terminations, many people miss the boat completely.

As a case in point, a company in my town treated an employee layoff as if it were a children's party game. One day, company representatives called a group of employees into the conference room and assigned them seats. The unsuspecting employees were then told to, at the same time, take the envelope from under their chair and keep it closed. They were advised to read it when they got home. Not everyone does what they are told, though, and several people opened their letters in the parking lot. Within twenty minutes, the press was there, and the now former employees were sharing their stories for all to hear.

Jeez, people. Where the heck is the compassion? The employees invited into that room weren't there for a birthday party; they were being sent home to loved ones or friends, whom they would have to inform that they would no longer be bringing home a paycheck. The handling of this layoff compounded an already difficult situation, and the emotional circus that followed the news could have easily been avoided had someone taken the time to consider whether the approach the company was about to take was respectful and compassionate.

Employee Terminations and Social Media

As if it weren't bad enough that you have to fire someone, now you also have to worry about him rating you on sites such as Glassdoor. Hell hath no fury like a terminated employee. If you don't believe me, check out all the negative online reviews people have written about their former employers. You just know they didn't leave of their own accord.

I believe you can significantly reduce this impact if you follow the suggestions I have offered above. I also recommend that you do whatever you can to provide a soft landing for those you are about to throw off the bus. Here are some suggestions for ways to soften the blow:

- Be generous with your severance. This is not the time to try and save a few bucks.
- When you are able, give the employee the option of resigning. Many will take you up on your offer, which will be a win-win for all involved.
- Provide assistance. This may be in the form of outplacement or additional money that the employee can use to retool her skill set.

As you can imagine, the topic of employee terminations is my least favorite area to write about, since it's a task that is emotionally draining and deeply impacts the lives of others. However, this is also the reason I have chosen to include this chapter in my book. If I can prevent just one employee from having an experience like some of the ones I've described, then my work is done here.

We've discussed what it takes to be a magnetic leader, including how to say goodbye to an employee in a way that is respectful and that reinforces your reputation as a leader who cares as deeply for his people (even those exiting) as he does for himself. In the next chapter, I'll show you how your own personal magnetism is directly connected to customer satisfaction and explosive growth.

Gravitational Pull Exercise #11

Jot down the names of those people who are no longer suited to your organization. Put together a transition plan and manage these people out. Do this today.

Part 3

Maximizing Your Magnetism

Chapter 12
The Magnetism Equation

People ask me all the time where I get my material. I can honestly say that I don't have to go far to find stories that are applicable to the topics I write about. In fact, today I didn't even have to leave my house. My downstairs neighbor sent me a text relaying her experience with a Bosch technician, who was at her home taking a look at her fairly new refrigerator. Here's how her text read, "I considered sending the Bosch technician up to you to interview for your book . . . he opened our fridge, declared it was working normally, then talked to me for twenty minutes about the management and infrastructure problems in his line of work." My sense is that she wasn't impressed. She has a full-time job, two young children, and a whole bunch of other stuff on her plate. The last thing she needs is to listen to someone else's woes. I'm pretty sure the company this guy works for is in need of a few (okay, a lot of) magnetic leaders.

I've never seen poorly managed employees provide high levels of service. Have you? Why should they bother? Who will really notice if they go all out to take care of a customer? You see this frequently in retail stores. Customers are drifting around aimlessly like Bedouins wandering in the desert while the staff is clustered behind the register complaining about management. One might ask, "Where the heck is the manager while all this is going on?" He is usually in the office scrolling the Internet in search of a new job while chatting on the phone with a friend.

It's interesting to me how this same scenario doesn't seem to be playing out at the Apple Store or your local Trader Joe's market. That's because they have what I call The Magnetism Equation going on. Here's the equation:

Magnetic Leadership + Incredible Customer Service = Explosive Growth

Walk into any Apple Store or Trader Joe's and you'll find management working side-by-side with their people. Speaking of people, grouchy employees need not apply for work with these companies, as they will not make it past the first round of interviews. In fact, a number of the leaders I interviewed for this book told me that the culture they've built ensures that those who don't fit in never make it in—and if they happen to somehow find their way into the organization, the organization expunges them. Employees who are a poor fit are either quickly terminated or they pack their bags and hit the trail in search of a company where slackers rarely get noticed.

The phrase "the customer experience" is bantered around a lot these days. And it should be, as this is the key to high levels of profitability. In particular, tech companies know that their customers are fickle and are more likely than those in other industries to move over to other products if they don't have a positive experience.

I myself am an example of how fickle a tech customer can be. I used to be loyal to Dell products. Every three years, like clockwork, I would order a new Dell laptop. Then, one day, something life changing happened—a new Apple store opened at my local mall. I'd walk by the store every week and watch all the people inside having what appeared to be a great time. I began to think about how I felt about my Dell experience. I never really had a great time with my Dell computer. That's probably because a good many of my days were spent with computer technician Dave, who was at my house fixing one computer problem or another. It was then that I made the decision to take a bite out of the big Apple.

Honestly, the pull was too great to resist. The people inside the store were nice, the product was awesome, and the service was irresistible. What more could a gal want? It's been well over ten years since my breakup with Dell, and not a day goes by that I don't think about how happy I am as an Apple customer. My family is now an Apple family, with the exception of my son, who keeps trying to convince me to go to the dark side, where gamers like him reside. No way, no how. Apple has taken a bite out of my heart and we are connected forever. That's how powerful The Magnetism Equation really is.

The Delightful Truth About Delighting Customers

How often does a friend brag about a restaurant experience that makes you feel the need to dash right over to OpenTable and snag a reservation? The answer, at least in my circle of friends, is lots! Remember when I said that great customer experiences are far and few these days? That's why when someone shares a delightful experience, we jump right in. And, of course, the restaurant business is all about the entire experience.

Several years ago I met Robert Irvine, of Restaurant Impossible fame, at Pizza Expo, where we were both speaking, and he said to me, "It doesn't matter how good the food at the restaurant is or the décor. If the service stinks, you're done for." I couldn't agree more. However, when the service is spectacular, it's quite another story. And, of course, there is no great service without great hires.

I recently dined at a restaurant called Siena in East Greenwich, Rhode Island, with a group of colleagues. We had an exceptional waitress who really knew her stuff. We ordered whatever she recommended and then we ordered more because she was so spot on with her recommendations. We left feeling quite full and satisfied, and we all vowed to return. I told others about our great evening and I'm sure my colleagues did the same. This delightful experience did not go unnoticed.

Now compare this to our experience just hours before at the hotel bar. My colleague Noah had looked at the cocktail menu and ordered a mojito. The waiter smiled and said, "Sorry, we don't have any mint." Noah and I looked at each other, and then I said, "I'm confused. There's a Stop and Shop Supermarket at the corner. Can't someone walk over there and get some?" The waiter's response basically indicated that he was unable to take matters into his own hands. Clearly, there was a management issue here. The waiter went on to say that they were in the process of changing over menus. In fact, he made it a point to tell us this at least three times. Noah then asked for the new cocktail menu, only to be told that it was not available yet. He leaned over to me and said, "Do you know what the difference is between an old menu and a new menu?" I said, "No." He said, "No menu!" The two of us simply could not believe the way this hotel bar was being run. We each vowed to make it the opening story for our next keynote. Believe me, this is not the kind of PR your organization would like to have.

When I look at the difference between these two experiences on that same night, I'm reminded of the importance of attracting the right people for the job you are trying to fill and being the type of leader who makes it possible for employees to delight the customer. Clearly, the waiter at the hotel bar wasn't the kind of employee who was used to *serving* the public, or he had been burnt one time too many by his boss when he was trying to delight a customer. The waitress at Siena was left to her own devices. She gladly poured tastes of the wines we were considering and probably would have been able to comp anything on the menu, had we not enjoyed everything. I suspect she works for a magnetic manager, as she has been working at that restaurant for quite a while. I just hope I can get a table at Siena, now that I've told you about the place!

Here's what happens when you have great employees working in concert with their leaders and one another to delight your clients and customers.

Nonstop Referrals

Here I am, telling all of you about this great restaurant that is located a bit off of the beaten trail. I tell all my friends about this place, and many drive right past hundreds of restaurants to get to this one. That's the power of referrals. Think about your own experiences and how many times you've referred people to your dentist, accountant, or one of your vendors, without having any of these people ask you to do so. And, of course, no conversation about referrals would be complete without a mention of social media. On these platforms, people are referring others to businesses 24-7. For me, referrals are the coinage of my business. I suspect it's the same for your business as well.

Nonprofits rely heavily on referrals for volunteers as well as when raising funds. Big Brothers, Big Sisters of Massachusetts Bay CEO Wendy Foster talked with me about the powerful connection between social media, referrals, and delighting volunteers, clients, and donors. Here's what she said: "When we delight people, it creates a buzz. People talk about us, and they talk about us to other people who are like them. Before we even get to the next person, they've already heard about us. They are warm and predisposed to us when they hear good things about our organization." She goes on to say, "That buzz creates momentum and there is a sense that your organization is on the move. People want to be associated with things that are noteworthy and organizations that are doing great things. Buzz creates momentum, which is a flywheel. It's like a gravitational force field. It attracts people forward."

More Forgiving Customers

I placed a call yesterday to Apple Care for help with my new iPad Pro. I was told the wait time would be longer than usual, something you tend to hear a lot these days on customer service lines. Seeing that it was the evening and I didn't have much else to do, I chose to wait. And then something really surprising happened. I was given the option of selecting the kind of music I wanted to listen to while on hold (you could also choose silence). I was be-bopping and rocking while on hold, listening to some pretty darn good music until my technician came on the line. He was polite and patient and quickly walked me through what I needed to do in order to get my new device in perfect working order. I've been on long holds more times than I can remember with my cable company, bank, and so on. Usually, by the time we are done with our call, I'm vowing to change vendors. Not so last night. I have such a strong pull to the Apple brand that I was willing to overlook the one time that I was on hold much longer than usual. I also have to admit, the awesome music selection certainly helped!

Reduction In Customer Acquisition Cost

If you've ever put pen to paper and figured out the cost of acquiring a customer, you'd be spending a heck of a lot more time trying to keep the customers you have. Naturally, customer acquisition costs vary depending on the product or service. However, the one thing that is constant is the fact that when clients or customers come to you, the cost of acquisition is significantly less than when you go to them. Here's where brand and reputation come into play.

A brand is nothing more than a promise. The one question I always ask prospects is, "What if your people can't keep your promise?" They usually say, "Tell me more." Throughout this book, I've discussed the importance of attracting and retaining the right talent, and how sometimes leaders repel talent without even knowing it. Your organization's ability to deliver on its promise to employees and customers is based on your actions as a leader. Those leaders who are able to hire and retain great brand ambassadors have customers wanting to do business with them because of their strong brand, which is naturally based on reputation.

We are all in the relationship business. People do business with people they like and respect. If customers like doing business with you, then they'll remain customers, which means you won't need to spend more money acquiring new clients to replace the ones you keep losing.

Happier and More Productive Employees and Customers

Has an unhappy employee ever waited on you? How did it feel? Not so great, right? I had such an experience this past winter. I had to dash into my local CVS Pharmacy to pick up a few items for my daughter on a snowy New England day. I about broke my neck as I slogged through the unplowed parking lot full of slush. Elderly people tend to visit drugstores, and this one was no exception. Concerned, I asked one of the clerks if she realized the parking lot hadn't been plowed. She looked at me with sad eyes and told me she already knew this. She went on to say that the manager didn't think it was necessary to call the plow service and she reminded me that she didn't have the authority to do so. I left, disappointed with her response and feeling like I needed to find a pharmacy that actually cared about the health and well-being of its customers *and* its employees.

I compare this to my experience at Whole Foods Market, where all I have to do is stare at a piece of unusual-looking fruit and a clerk is right there to slice it open and provide me with a sample. The cheerful clerks have me coming back time after time with little regard for the fact that I may be paying more than if I shopped at my local food store. For me and others, it's about the experience. That darn store is like a magnet. It pulls me in. That's the kind of connection you want your customers to have to you. When the pull is that strong, costs become secondary.

Reduced Stress

Let's face it, when things are going well, stress levels tend to stay in check. Employees are happy and they stick around; clients are satisfied and refer others; revenues are up; profits are soaring. Life is good! It's great when you have the resources you need to reinvest in the business. You can sit back and reap the benefits that come with success, and you don't have to spend your discretionary income on services that are meant to reduce your stress.

More Revenue

Think for a moment. What is the happiest place on earth? If you guessed one of the Disney theme parks, you are correct. Some say it's harder to get a job in the Disney College Program than it is to get accepted at Harvard. Disney is completely focused on the customer experience, and company managers realize that the only way they can deliver this consistently is by hiring those who love the fairy tale as much as they do. Once inside the park, visitors throw caution (and their budgets) to the wind. As a visitor, I've experienced smiling employees telling me how cute my daughter looked in the $20 Disney princess crown she was trying on. I gladly handed over my credit card. I know people who make annual meccas to Disney, and many of these people no longer have kids living at home. I suspect they go for the memories, and many wind up taking their grandchildren as well. Disney is a brand that never seems to disappoint. The streets are lined with gold, and rivers of revenue streams wind through the park. In fact, the Walt Disney Company posted *record-breaking* profits in its fiscal first quarter of 2016.

Increased Profits and Possibilities

When you've achieved this level of magnetism, profits soon follow, and so do possibilities. You have the resources to invest in new products or services. Acquisitions and business growth are real possibilities. And with growth comes the opportunity to provide more career options to those in your employ, which adds to the stickiness you've been working so hard to create.

As you can see, everything comes full circle as a direct result of the shift that occurs when you permit yourself to become a magnetic leader. The return on your efforts will certainly be rewarding, both personally and professionally.

Everyone's a Critic

You used to have to worry about someone speaking badly of you at a cocktail party or prospects reading a terrible review in the local newspaper or seeing negative comments in a trade journal. These days, everyone is a critic. Customers are writing reviews, in real time, from the palm of their hands on popular websites such as Yelp and Angie's List. It seems like no one can escape this ratings craze, including customers, who these days are being rated by their Uber drivers!

I remember the first time this happened to me. I had called for an Uber, and the driver who picked me up commented on my great rating. Confused, I asked him how I could possibly even have a rating since this was my first time using the service. He smiled and said that everyone starts out with a five star rating. It was at that point that I realized my rating could only go in one direction—down. As I reflected on this, I wondered why I would even care what Uber's drivers think of me. I then learned that if I got a bad reputation as a patron, I might be left by the side of the road with all the other badly behaving customers, hoping and praying that I could get a ride in an old-fashioned taxi, where no one really cares about your rating—or about service.

Say you are in a restaurant with some friends and your food arrives. It used to be that you wait until everyone was served before you began eating. Now you have to wait until everyone has taken photos and posted them to Instagram or Facebook before you can enjoy your meal. After-dinner drinks are now accompanied by the posting of a review on OpenTable, Yelp, or UrbanSpoon. There is no longer room for error or rude employees. The opposite holds true as well. Exceptional customer experiences, accompanied by glowing reviews, mean a dramatic increase in orders, reservations, and profits!

Everyone Gets a Vote

When did the workplace become a democracy? I get the sense that employers are afraid to make a move without having employees vote on the matter at hand. This probably explains why employees are spending about half their workdays in meetings, costing companies billions in lost productivity. I understand the need to collaborate when the work requires it—for example, when a team is designing a new product—but all too often the company is seeking opinions for fear that the organization might receive negative comments from its own employees on platforms like Glassdoor, a website that features more than eight million company reviews posted by current and prospective employees as well as former workers.

That said, people who are looking at Glassdoor comments could very well veer away from your product or service based on what they are reading. For example, suppose you are considering doing business with a company that will also be servicing the product you will be buying. You go onto Glassdoor, and the first thing you read is that this company cannot keep technicians. You may very well think twice before choosing this vendor, especially if you value a long-term relationship with the person who will be responsible for maintaining your account. You can also get a good sense of how engaged a particular company's employees are, based on the comments on Glassdoor. If you are looking at making a capital investment, you would certainly think twice about doing so with a company who looks like it could go under any day based on the comments you are reading online from its employees.

I'm hard pressed to think of one area these days where the layperson's opinion doesn't count. And if the opinion is on the Internet, then of course it must be true. This is a huge problem for leaders and organizations that aren't monitoring their social media platforms. You simply can no longer ignore these channels, and if you choose to do so, it's at your own peril.

How to Rewrite Your Story

Like I said, there are no secrets anymore. It's not only right to treat your employees as well as you treat customers; it's also the only way to act these days, especially if you value your reputation and are interested in long-term profitable growth. Now go over to Glassdoor.com and see what people are saying about your company. If it's not the message you want them to be conveying, then vow to rewrite your story. Begin with the following exercise:

- What do you want people to say about your style of leadership and the company you represent?
- What they are saying now?
- Where are the gaps?

Focus on the areas that will have the greatest impact. When you are doing this exercise, it's important to allow yourself to be vulnerable. It's not easy to listen to negative feedback, particularly when it's about you. Accept that what is being said is that person's perception, which is their reality. Now think about what you need to do to change the perception. It is possible if you are willing to do the internal work necessary to improve. Just ask PANALITIX CEO Rob Nixon, who went from repelling talent to having a business that is inspirational, a team with energy and a big vision. "People want to be part of something great," notes Nixon. That includes employees and customers as well.

You understand by now the power associated with magnetic leadership. In this next chapter, we'll discuss how your magnetism can propel your personal brand forward.

Gravitational Pull Exercise #12

Begin rewriting your story. Start by keeping the end in mind. As a leader, what would you like your legacy to be? What steps do you need to take in order to get there? Then make it so.

Chapter 13
From "Who?" to an Unforgettable You

Quick, write down the names of all the managers you've ever worked for. Do this in less than twenty seconds. Who topped your list and whom did you forget? Those you remembered left some sort of impression—hopefully, a good one. We used to call this your reputation. Now it's called your personal brand. It communicates the value you offer.

In the old days, say, five years ago, not much attention was paid to personal brands. You did your job and didn't give much thought about the way others perceived you, unless you worked for an organization where promotions were mostly based on office politics. As I mentioned in chapter 12, everyone's opinion seems to count these days, hence my desire to include a discussion on the connection between personal magnetism, your personal brand, and why you should pay attention to all of this.

Regardless of your official title, keep in mind that you are the CEO of Brand You. That means you are in charge of managing your personal brand, so that others view exactly as you want them to. Here's how your own personal magnetism can help propel both your personal brand and your career forward.

The Power of a Strong Personal Brand

Picture a CEO at the head of a conference room table with her trusted executives close by, discussing whom to promote into the newly created VP position. Is it coincidence that the usual suspects are suggested by more than one person in the room, or do these people happen to have strong personal brands that keep their names front and center? I'm betting it's the latter.

I have found that too many people shy away from self-promotion. They think performance alone will get them to the top. Sorry, folks, but that's not even true in Hollywood. I was teaching a class on executive presence for women in tech, and when I stressed this point about self-promotion I made a number of people quite uncomfortable. I'm okay with that, for discomfort leads to growth. Failing to self-promote is a critical mistake that needs to be avoided at all costs. Why? There is no point in being a best-kept secret. Many artists never achieved fame until they passed. I don't know about you, but I certainly don't want to wait until I'm long gone before others hear about my contributions. The world of business is competitive, and if you want to thrive you need to take a more active role in your own promotion. I'll teach you how to do this shortly. However, before we begin, I want to be sure you understand why all this matters.

Ease of Recruitment

You'll never be able to compete for talent using money. That's because there will always be someone who has the means to pay people more money than you are willing or able to pay them. As we've discussed, your ability to fill open positions will dramatically improve as your pull gets stronger. You'll also find that people will follow you from one company to another, thereby enabling you to focus on results while others are struggling to get by with unfilled job openings. Your performance will soar, which leads to our next reason that personal magnetism matters.

Plum Assignments

The quickest way to propel your career forward is to be assigned high-profile projects. It might be a project personally sanctioned by the CEO or a highly visible initiative that will be watched closely by many. Plum assignments are given to those who can be trusted to successfully complete the work. Trust is based on reputation. See where I'm going with this?

It's up to you to make sure others know you are the right person for the task at hand. That's where strategic bragging comes in. Highlight something about your background that makes you a person of interest. You weave this into the conversation, which helps you quickly build trust and rapport, which in turn pulls people toward you.

Here's an example of strategic bragging. Suppose you are fluent in Japanese and your company is about to open an office in Japan. You might casually mention your facility with the language when you are discussing the expansion plans with the executive team. Here's what this conversation might sound like: "You know, when I lived in Japan, back in the late nineties, we had to speak Japanese in order to be served, especially when we were in remote areas of the country. We also had to quickly come up to speed on the cultural differences, so that we'd be accepted by the locals." There. You've just become a person of interest who is now on everyone's radar to be part of the international team that will open up this promising new market.

Increased Employee Retention

Who doesn't want to be near someone who exudes kinetic energy? I remember in graduate school sitting next to a colleague whose magnetism I could feel. It wasn't long before we became great friends, and we remain close today. This woman is a leader of a Fortune 500 company, and those who are lucky enough to earn a spot in her department remain there. That's the power of personal brand and magnetism. And again, think of all the great work a leader is able to do when she oversees a well-trained team who knows what the other members are thinking before anyone even speaks. The team has been together for a long time and they are able to successfully take on complex assignments because of their synergy. Compare this to the leader in the next cube, who is in a constant state of chaos because she must constantly replace people who leave faster than she can bring them in. Now, who do you think will receive the larger bonus or the next opportunity that comes along?

Promotions

At the end of the day, most people are working to advance their careers. Naturally, those with strong personal brands are the first names to come up when discussions regarding promotions take place. I asked you earlier to take twenty seconds to write down the names of all the people you've ever worked for. Now I'm going to ask you to take the next twenty seconds and write down the names of everyone who currently works for you. Whose name did you think of first? Most likely, it's the employee who is your go-to person. If a promotion comes along, it's going to this person, right? Is he the most qualified person for the job? Maybe. What really matters most is that he is top of mind.

Premium Wages

It's great to be in demand, isn't it? You can pretty much write your own ticket. Headhunters and company recruiters are regularly contacting those with strong brands. The first question that is asked is, "What will it take to get you to make a move?" Only a fool would say, "You'd have to match my salary." Instead, you'd think of a much larger number than your current compensation and you'd toss that number out there, especially if you weren't actively seeking a new job. If your reputation in the industry is particularly strong, you know you can suggest an even higher number than you could if you were unknown.

It's not unheard of for magnetic leaders to be involved in bidding wars for their talent. It happens all the time in the world of sports as well as in the executive suite and other parts of organizations. You'll be in the best position if you have a strong brand both internally and externally. Where you go from there is all up to you, as you'll have lots of options to choose from.

Remaining in Place

What if you are at the point in your career where you are happy where you are and you are no longer interested in new opportunities? Should you simply dismiss this idea of a personal brand? Not if you want to keep your job. "Safe" jobs disappear daily, as do entire departments. To increase the likelihood that you'll be able to remain where you currently are, you'll need to amplify your brand so that you remain on the "keeper" list. However, you may not need to invest as much effort in branding as those who are still looking to make some solid career moves.

Brand You

Everyone has a brand, even if your brand right now is somewhat generic because you aren't standing out in the crowd. That's okay. It is certainly a better position to be in than having a brand that is tainted. Here's where to begin when creating Brand You.

Start with the end goal in mind. Take a piece of paper and write down your response to the following questions. I recommend making notes on paper rather than on your computer so you don't get distracted by incoming e-mail or the latest scores from today's game. When responding to these questions, write down everything that comes to mind. Don't filter your thoughts; just write them. When you are done, go back and look for patterns.

Ten Questions to Help You Create a Personal Magnetic Brand

1. How would I like to be remembered?
2. What's my purpose, both professionally and personally?
3. What would I like employees, customers, clients, and others to say about me when I'm not in the room?
4. What are some things that most people don't know about me that would enhance my magnetism?
5. What do I do better than anyone else?
6. If I could only receive one award in my lifetime, what would that be?
7. What do people most compliment me on?
8. What adjectives do people use when introducing me to others?
9. What am I expert at or renowned for?
10. What makes me unique compared to my peers?

If you've done this correctly, you'll see that you do indeed have a brand. If you are unable to answer these questions yourself, ask people who know you well for some help. This includes friends, relatives, peers, your boss, employees, vendors, and clients. You may not be thrilled with all the answers you receive, but at least you'll have a starting point to build upon.

Selling You

Now that you've established your personal brand, you'll need to take this to market. That means that you'll need to sell yourself so that you aren't the world's best-kept secret. Marketing experts will tell you that the key to a strong brand is consistency. That's why you don't see bottles of Pepsi dressed up in different colors (unless of course it's a special occasion) or McDonald's fast food restaurants looking all that different around the globe.

A good place to start is with your LinkedIn profile, as many companies are turning to LinkedIn for their recruitment needs. It's also the place where you can shamelessly promote yourself without much effort or criticism. To create a powerful LinkedIn profile, pay special attention to the following:

- **Your picture.** A picture is worth a thousand words. There is a time and a place for selfies. This isn't it. Invest in a professional headshot.
- **Your headline.** Picking an attractive headline is more challenging then creating a tweet. With Twitter you get 140 characters to work with; LinkedIn only gives you 120 characters to create interest. Your headline needs to reflect the brand you are trying to create. Choose descriptive and compelling words.
- **Summary.** Think of this as a sixty-second commercial that presents an overview of yourself. That's not a lot of time to grab people's attention and have them wanting more after. Be pithy. Be interesting. Be yourself.
- **Experience.** Don't copy and paste your resume here. Instead, share specifics regarding the outcomes you've achieved in the positions you've held. Keep in mind that the goal is to become a person of interest.
- **Recommendations.** If you can easily get them, great! But I wouldn't waste hours trying to get these, as few people actually read them.
- **Stay up to date.** Be sure to keep your LinkedIn profile updated. Keep adding content and reaching out to those who look like they might be an interesting connection.

If you've recently completed a milestone, such as earning a master's degree, then you'll want to be sure you notify your HR department so they can update your profile in the company Human Resource Information System (HRIS). Companies tend to rely on these systems for succession planning or when searching for internal candidates, prior to going to the outside market.

You'll also want to craft your elevator pitch. An elevator pitch is what you'll say when you meet people at networking events or neighborhood barbeques. This is a brief statement about you, meant to entice others to continue having a conversation with you. Try and stay away from the more traditional and sometimes repellent lines such as, "I sell life insurance," unless of course your aim is to be left alone! The more interesting your pitch is, the better. All you really want someone to do is say, "Tell me more."

Speak everywhere you can, whenever the opportunity presents itself, whether that is to a college club filled with students or an industry association meeting. The point is to be sure you are being viewed as an expert in your field. Everyone wants to be affiliated with experts and thought leaders. Be that person.

Get involved in an industry association. Better yet, take on a leadership role in the association, which will provide you with even greater visibility. The more visible you are, the more likely people will come to you with opportunities. In addition, those who are seeking new job opportunities will come to you for advice, which will give you first dibs on talent.

Coauthor a paper or write a book. Again, the idea is to draw people toward you, which is what magnetism is all about.

Affiliate with others who have strong brands. In marketing, product placement is everything. The same holds true with personal brands. Presenting on the same stage as someone who is well known automatically makes you a person of interest. Now you need to leverage this by notifying your social network and others of this exciting news. You can also drop it into conversations. For example, I'll often say to people, "When Bill O'Reilly and I were discussing sex in the workplace, we talked about. . ." Boom! Now your brand is even stronger because you've subtly let others know that the media relies on you for expert advice. Note that before this television appearance, I had no idea I was an expert on sex in the workplace, but apparently I am! Why else would they ask me to speak with the Fox News Network's infamous Bill O'Reilly on such a compelling topic?

Being Memorable

There is so much noise in every channel these days. That's why I tell my clients to find a lane that is not occupied and make it your own. You can do this by looking into the future and asking yourself:

- What are the trends shaping my industry?
- What kind of impact will these trends have on the status quo?
- What can I do today to ensure I'm the go-to person of tomorrow?
- What do I need to get better at in order to be known as a thought leader in my field and in my industry?
- Who should I affiliate with in order to elevate my brand?

Take, for example, the title of chief customer officer. This position is a relatively new position that has come into existence to help organizations maximize customer acquisition, retention, and profitability. Those who were able to anticipate a need for someone with this breadth of skills were well situated to take on these roles, while others are still trying to catch up. By the time they do, there may very well be an entirely new set of skills needed for a role that has yet to be defined.

Pay close attention to trends in your field so you can determine what's next. By doing this, you'll be able to create a powerful personal brand that will ensure you are front and center when opportunity presents itself.

Leveraging Your Unique Strengths

Think about how you might be different from the rest of the crowd. For example, suppose you are a software engineer who happens to have strong communications skills. The combination of technical expertise and the ability to speak to customers in a way that does not sound like techno babble to them is rare and can certainly elevate your personal brand, keeping you in high demand. Those strong communication skills will also come in handy should you decide to lead a team of engineers or technical salespeople.

If you are unable to assess what makes you different (in a good way) from your peers, find someone who can help you gather this information. Companies do this type of market research all the time for their products and services. You'll benefit from doing such research as well. Hire a coach who can do a 360 assessment, which involves gathering feedback from your managers, peers, and direct reports. This person may even speak with vendors and customers. Having a clear picture of how others view you can help you build your personal brand more effectively. The information you collect will help to ensure that you are working on the right things rather than everything.

Truth in Advertising

It's important to make sure all aspects of your personal brand are consistent across all channels and attract the right attention to you. Many of my clients have started to blog, which is a great way to build thought leadership and to attract others to you. Some are writing columns for a local business journal, while others are taking leadership positions in industry associations to better position themselves.

Check your Twitter, Facebook, and LinkedIn profiles to ensure the brand you are working so hard to build won't come crashing down with one wrong tweet or ill-advised post. For example, if you are working diligently to build the image of a responsible leader, make sure images posted on Facebook of you doing Jell-O shots at a party aren't visible for all to see. Facebook is notorious for changing its privacy settings frequently. Be sure to check your privacy settings often. Manage your social media channels yourself to ensure that your messaging is pure and that what you are putting out there is what you want people to see.

Be authentic. The goal here is to attract the *right* people to you for the *right* reasons. Baiting and switching will result in damage to both your personal brand and that of the company. Here's what I mean by this: I had lunch with a friend today who told me the story of her friend, who had left a good job for the promise of a better job and a nice bump in pay. Her new boss promised her the sun, the moon, the stars, and flexible work hours—something that was very important to this single mom. She was barely on the job a week when she realized she'd been had. All the money in the world could not make up for the stress she was feeling trying to make it home in time to meet her child's school bus. She immediately started looking for a new job, and within three months she was gone. So was the personal brand of the leader who was dishonest in his dealings with her.

There are plenty of people out there who can work long hours for the right deal. Clearly, this woman was unable to do so and had even mentioned this to the hiring manager during her interview with him. That's what I mean when I say that you need to hire the right people for the right reasons. Had this leader done so, he might still have a great employee singing his praises for all to hear.

Making Your Magnetism Personal

Commune Hotels CEO Niki Leondakis is a fine example of using one's personal brand to change the world, even if that change comes one woman at a time. Leondakis is on the board of Dress for Success, an organization whose mission is to empower women to achieve economic independence by providing a network of support, professional attire, and the development tools women need to thrive in work and in life. "I'm passionately involved with Dress for Success and have been for over ten years. We are helping women become financially independent," states Leondakis. She believes it's her civic and social responsibility to help people in need and to inspire others to make the world a better place. She's able to do this because of her strong personal brand. "I've leveraged the platform that I'm on to benefit society by bringing my team to help with the cause I'm passionately involved with," she says.

I've seen other magnetic leaders do this as well. Whenever leaders ask me to pitch in for a cause they believe in or to attend an event that's being put on by an organization they support, I'm there! The room is usually filled with members of their staff who are thrilled to be attending such highly visible events and to be seen doing so with their leader.

As you can see, the strength of magnetism goes beyond improving organizations, attracting customers, and increasing profits. A strong platform can open doors for you and can be fulfilling both professionally and personally. What are you waiting for? Pick one or two areas to focus on, and you'll be well on your way to creating a magnetic brand that will make you memorable.

Gravitational Pull Exercise #13

Write down your answers to the ten questions that elaborate how to create a personal magnetic brand. Then pump up the volume so that you can be heard in a sea of cubicles.

Chapter 14
Perpetual Magnetism:
Sustaining Your Leadership Charge

How long can you go without charging your cell phone before it dies? Your iPad? Probably not all that long. The same rules apply to sustaining your magnetic charge. The number of people who choose to subscribe to my free newsletter, *The Talent Maximizer*®, in any given week is directly related to how often I'm posting to my *Forbes* blog and my personal blog. When I increase my social media interactions, I immediately see an uptick in the number of people who are following me. Sometimes I get lazy or I'm too busy to do a lot of writing or marketing. As a result, my business tends to slow in direct proportion to the slowdown in my marketing efforts.

The same things happens with your magnetism. Some of you may be all charged up after reading this book and will head out of the gate with the commitment of an Olympian who has one shot to score gold. I'm going to suggest that you pull the reins back a bit so that you can stay in control of your efforts. Magnetism is a long-term commitment that requires charging every now and again. If you fail to internalize your learning and apply these concepts daily, you'll no doubt run out of steam and connectivity.

Like many of you, I've been a leader in the C-suite and understand the pressures of meeting short-term goals, time and time again. As I look back, I can honestly say one of my biggest mistakes was not taking time for my own renewal. If we are being truthful here, I thought I was hot stuff and didn't need to do much work on myself. After all, I was twenty-four years old and running my own department in a prestigious company!

What I've learned over the years, having worked with hundreds of leaders, is that it's critical to give oneself permission to take the time necessary to allow good habits to develop. That's why all my coaching projects include a maintenance period, where we work together to ensure the changes we've worked to achieve can be sustained over time.

It's important to remember that we are looking for *long-term* results here—not just a temporary change in behavior. This huge shift will allow you to continue to attract more qualified employees, better customers, and nonstop revenue!

Keeping the Forces Alive

It's important to understand that your magnetism will vary. You'll have days when it feels like the world is in love with you and you'll have to ward people off, and there will be other times when you'll feel like the least popular guy on the block. All of this comes with the territory.

Keep doing what I've suggested you do, and eventually this will even out. Here's why: if you do as I've suggested, you'll have much stronger relationships with team members and others in the organization. This means that if you make a small mistake, most likely it's not going to cost you everything you've worked so hard to build. People will be more willing to overlook a few missteps here and there, especially when they have a high level of respect and admiration for the person who seems to be having an off day.

There will be times when you may feel as if you are putting in a lot of effort and you aren't reaping much in return. Be patient. Becoming magnetic is a lot like creating a garden. In the beginning, it feels like a lot of work. You have to choose your plot, turn the soil, add nutrients to the soil, select the seeds or plants, put them in the ground, and take special care to ensure the weeds aren't encroaching on your plants. You water the garden daily, and on most days you don't really notice much of a difference. You step away for several days to tend to other matters and when you return, voila! Your efforts are rewarded with an abundance of color and bounty. The same will happen with your magnetism. You'll go from unknown to renowned in what appears to others to be over-night success. Of course, you and I will know that the care and attention you've been investing into growing your personal brand has finally yielded the results you've worked so hard to achieve. Enjoy the bounty!

Staying Charged

One of the best ways to keep your magnetic charge is to hang out with like-minded people. These are leaders who are similar to you in that they are looking to improve everyday. They are willing to challenge themselves to be better than they even thought was possible.

Consider starting a Magnetic Leader mastermind group. Mastermind groups offer a combination of brainstorming, education, peer accountability, and support in a group setting, allowing you to sharpen your business and personal skills. Over the years, I've been part of several mastermind groups, and I can personally attest to the power of a mastermind group as a means to achieve success.

Participants challenge group members to set powerful goals and, more importantly, to accomplish them. They support you when you are down and they are there to celebrate with you when things are going well. Like any group, the particular members you invite to join matter. That's why I'm suggesting that you start your own group rather than joining one that's already in progress. By doing so, you can retain control over the membership roster. I'm not trying to be a snob here. I know from my own experience that even one member who isn't the right fit can have a negative impact on the results group members achieve. And because it's your group, I'm assuming you want to maximize your experience.

If you want to improve more rapidly, consider bringing in an outside facilitator who can keep the group on track. As part of my practice I've put together group coaching programs for magnetic leaders, which operate in a similar manner to a mastermind group. The big difference is that members have direct access to me, so they needn't be burdened with the process of assembling a group themselves and they don't have to worry about logistics. I always consider if the person will fit and do not hesitate to turn away those who would not add value to the group.

For those of you who aren't joiners, I recommend finding an accountability partner. This is someone you can count on to help you stay on track. I have an accountability partner who I met through my mastermind group. While we still participate in the group, we frequently have side conversations that allow us to challenge one another, as not every matter we have requires the expertise of the entire group. What I like most about this type of relationship is that we have similar practices, only on different sides of the country. We never hesitate to call each other out on something one of us may be doing that we know darn well isn't helping to move us forward.

Personally, I don't care if you choose to work in a group or with one other person. I know from own my experience the importance of surrounding yourself with supportive people. These people need to have your best interest in mind. As a result, they will be honest and committed, and they will maintain confidentiality. They'll also be your biggest cheerleaders.

Challenging the Status Quo

Here you are. You've done all the work to become one of those leaders others aspire to be. It's easy to shift into automatic pilot when things seem to be humming along. This is a mistake only amateurs make. To maintain your personal attraction and to continue growing as a leader, you have to be willing to put yourself out there. This means challenging the status quo. I strongly suggest you eliminate the words "That's the way we've always done things" from your vocabulary. Leaders in search of personal improvement understand that if you are not moving forward, you are falling behind.

Here's an example of how challenging the status quo can help you retain your magnetic status. Suppose it's become common in your organization for the CFO to approve all salary increases. He has the authority to approve or disapprove of a salary increase for one of your employees, whom he doesn't even know. Typically, the CFO bounces back all recommendations for increases that are higher than what is given to an average employee. Your employee is anything but average, so you decide to challenge the status quo. You go to the CEO to present your case for why involving the CFO in every salary decision no longer makes sense. The CEO agrees and gives you, the director, approval to use your salary budget as you see fit. You now are able to provide your most valuable employee with the level of raise you so strongly feel she deserves.

Believe me when I tell you that the employee who is about to receive a raise larger than most will know that you've gone to bat for her. Although we'd like to think that salaries are confidential, in my experience, this is rarely the case! This employee will remain attached to you and will be singing your praises for years to come.

Improving Yourself by 2 Percent Every Day

I used to have a personal trainer come to my house weekly. It wasn't long before I had built up some amazing upper body strength. Then life got crazy. My husband and I built a house, but things didn't go according to plan. We packed up two high school–aged children and moved them from the country to the city. And to add more fuel to the fire, the house we thought we'd sell in a month is still on the market. We've spent the past year in building hell, dealing with all the turmoil of a project that went south.

The money I used to pay my personal trainer is now being spent to recover from our transition. My amazing muscle mass has gone on hiatus. This is what happens when you stop investing in yourself. You lose muscle mass.

Achieving your desired state is only half the equation. That's why weight-loss leaders like Weight Watchers have maintenance programs. It can be more challenging to maintain your status than to achieve your goal. Why? Because you are no longer able to easily see and measure progress. But don't be fooled; every day you are able to maintain your status is a day of progress, and one worth celebrating. The same holds true when it comes to attracting others toward you. This means that you are reaping the benefits of magnetism, both from a professional and personal point of view, even if you don't necessarily feel like much progress is really happening.

Here are some ways you can improve by 2 percent every day to maintain your magnetic charge.

Be a Mentor

I have found that one of the best ways to remain on top of my game is to mentor others. Here's why. My mentees may ask me something that

I don't have an immediate answer for, which means that I have to do some research. This research always results in my learning something new and valuable. They also challenge me to look at situations from a different perspective. And, most importantly, my understanding of leadership deepens when I'm sharing my expertise with others. In fact, there have been many times when I believe I've learned more from them than they've learned from me.

Take Time Out for Learning

Make it a point to find a conference that is worth your time. Notice that I didn't say worth your money. Your time is valuable. If you are going to take time away from the office, you want to be sure you'll have ample opportunity to mingle with the right people, including the thought leaders who are presenting. You may even want to reach out to some of the speakers before the conference to see if they are amenable to meeting for coffee either before or after their session. This personal relationship building may lead to other opportunities for you.

Stay Current on Leadership Trends

Sign up for a subscription to the *Harvard Business Review* or another publication of your choosing, so that you can stay abreast of the latest research on business and leadership. Share relevant articles with other leaders in your organization, particularly those leaders you are responsible for developing.

Don't Be Afraid to Fail

I encounter leaders who are prolific readers of business books, yet they don't seem to be applying what they are learning to their own situations. When I ask why this is so, I get answers like, "What if this doesn't work?" "What if I get it wrong? "I'm not ready yet. I need more time." My mentor Alan Weiss always says, "If you are not failing, you are not trying." I couldn't agree more. He also says, "Look, we are not fighting a war here, although some days it might certainly feel like we are. No one is shooting at us. What's the worst thing that can happen?" I believe the worst thing that can happen is that we do nothing. When we do nothing, things never improve, and if we aren't improving, we are falling behind. I suggest you apply what you are learning and make adjustments as you move ahead. You are going to make mistakes. That's a given. Learn from your mistakes so that you don't repeat them.

Stay Connected

As you rise through the ranks, you'll find it harder to stay connected with those who matter most—the people who have direct contact with your customers. With all that technology has to offer today, there is no longer an excuse for being out of touch. At Yelp, CEO Jeremy Stopple-man does video blogs weekly. "Engagement is about cadence, getting the right message to the people when they need it most, not when you most need it," notes YELP VP of corporate communications Shannon Eis. You do this through a series of channels, which, depending on your culture, may include YouTube or weekly chats on Google Hangouts or Skype. Not only is engagement about cadence; magnetism is as well. Don't let your tech skills hold you back from remaining connected. A good old-fashioned handwritten note never goes out of style and will certainly help you stand out these days.

Keep Your Energy Level High

It's hard to remain excited about working for a leader who appears to be somewhat exhausted. Whether you like it or not, you are a role model. Your energy is contagious—and your lack of enthusiasm is too. "There are certain times and opportunities where I really focus on amping up my energy!" exclaims Big Brothers Big Sisters of Mas-sachusetts Bay CEO Wendy Foster. "You really have to project it out to the world, and I'm conscious of the times that I need to really boost my magnetism. I may be speaking in a room full of nine hundred people or trying to get my point across at a staff meeting," Foster says. Understanding when you need to dial your energy level up and when you should ratchet it down comes with experience. When in doubt, choose enthusiasm!

Sticking to Your Commitment

When I met with Harpoon Brewery CEO Dan Kenary, he mentioned something that has stuck in my head. He said, "Millennials won't tolerate the disconnect between values and the company. Treat others as you'd like to be treated yourself." He went on to say, "You have to be committed to doing this day in and day out. You cannot take your foot off the pedal."

Look, you're going to have some days when you think, why the heck can't I just manage people like people were managed in the old days, back when you gave people an order and then you used your stick to ensure they carried out your order properly. I suppose you could try that approach, although I'm fairly certain it wouldn't be long before employees grabbed your stick and used it on you. Of course, the whole scene would be recorded on someone's phone and be up on YouTube before you could say the words, "My bad."

Leadership is a journey. You'll have some good days and some days that, quite frankly, you'll hope to never have again. When you hit your stride, you'll know it.

Charging Up Your Followers

Ultimately, we are responsible for bringing along the next generation of leaders. Most are opening to learning and are looking forward to their next promotion. However, they can't grow as leaders if we don't give them the freedom to fail. Unfortunately, many are not accustomed to failure. Helicopter parents—those who hover over their child's every move—have raised a number of your younger followers. Those parents were there to pick their kids up when they fell and cheer them on in spite of a disastrous performance. Their cherubs are now in your charge. Many have never received constructive feedback, which means you may very well be the first to tell them that their leadership style might not be as perfect as they think. This fact shouldn't deter you from being honest with them. However, you may want to tread lightly until they've had an opportunity to develop tougher skin.

It shouldn't be that difficult to keep your followers charged up if you show them that you have their best interest at heart. If you are constantly modeling the behaviors we've talked about throughout this book, then your followers will have a great role model. Your magnetic charge will rub off on them, hopefully right around the time it's their turn to carry the leadership torch.

My hope is that one day you'll be considered in such high regard as Raymond Pawlicki, former CIO of Biogen. His magnetism lives on in spite of the fact that he's retired. His pull remains strong, and as a result he's been invited to sit on several boards. His magnetism has catapulted him into an entirely new universe, one that he certainly appears to be enjoying.

At the end of most people's careers, they retire. For the magnetic leader, retirement is an interim step with endless possibilities. It's that charge that catapults you way beyond what you ever imagined was even possible.

Gravitational Pull Exercise #14

What, specifically, are you willing to commit to in order to sustain your personal magnetism? Find an accountability partner and share your list with her. Ask this person to help you stay on track.

Conclusion

At the beginning of this book, I talked about how employees don't work for companies; they work for people. Clients and customers also choose to work with you and your organization (or they choose not to) based on the experience they have with your people. If the experience is favorable, they'll recommend you to others, which is the lowest cost of customer acquisition possible. If the experience is not a happy one, they'll warn everyone they know never to do business with you, which could result in your company going out of business. You can see clearly how profits are directly tied to leadership, and that your connection to your employees is the beginning of a chain of experiences that directly impacts the bottom line of your organization.

If you take only one thing away from this book, let it be that the *way* you choose to lead matters more than your intentions, and that every day is a new opportunity to lead in a way that is memorable for the right reasons. My hope is that you have already begun to view your role as a leader differently than you might have when you first picked up this book.

As you move forward, keep in mind that leadership is a journey, while management is more like a destination. Understanding this difference is important. Many people achieve the status of manager, and once they've done so they feel they've arrived. They lose all sense of curiosity and are satisfied with the status quo. They don't look to improve, nor do they seek other pastures. They remain in place, where hopefully they do no harm.

On the journey to leadership, you'll travel from one place to another. Some locations will be more exotic than others. There will be times when you take the direct route and other times when you decide the scenic route is in order. You'll meet all types of people along the way, and they will enrich the experience. There will be times when you are simply exhausted and other moments when your breath is taken away by what's in front of you. You may scale some very large mountains and you may inadvertently roll down some hills. When you look back you will be amazed by what you were able to achieve, especially when you realize that you have touched people's lives in ways you couldn't have imagined were possible.

I'll be the first to admit that what I've discussed throughout this book isn't rocket science. Rocket science is logical and somewhat predictable. Those who understand rocket science and have chosen to take us to worlds unknown simply amaze me.

Leadership is exactly the opposite of rocket science, and for many it's just as complex. It's unpredictable and at times highly illogical. It's the thrill and excitement that have led me down this path of helping leaders like you find their magnetism. The truth is, magnetism was inside you all along. I just helped pull it out of you and escorted you on this part of your journey. I hope you will do the same for those you lead.

I'm glad I've been able to join you on this part of your leadership transformation. E-mail me at Roberta@matusonconsulting.com and let me know how you are doing on your voyage to becoming a magnetic leader and if I can be of help. Where you go from here is entirely up to you. From my vantage point, the sky is the limit!

References

Arum, Richard, and Josipa Roksa. *Academically Adrift: Limited Learning on College Campuses*. Chicago: University of Chicago Press, 2011.

Bureau of Labor Statistics. "Census of Fatal Occupational Injuries (CFOI)." http://www.cdc.gov/niosh/topics/violence/.

Bureau of Labor Statistics, U.S. Department of Labor. "Employee Tenure Summary." http://www.bls.gov/news.release/tenure.nr0.htm.

CareerBuilder. "2015 CareerBuilder Candidate Behavior Study." http://www.careerbuildercommunications.com/candidatebehavior/.

CareerBuilder. "Workers Name Their Top Office Romance Deal Breakers in New Career-Builder Survey." http://www.careerbuilder.com/share/aboutus/pressreleasesdetail.aspx?sd=2%2F11%2F2015&id=pr868&ed=12%2F31%2F2015.

Deloitte. "Deloitte Millennial Survey." http://www2.deloitte.com/content/dam/Deloitte/global/Documents/About-Deloitte/gx-dttl-2014-millennial-survey-report.pdf.

Deloitte. "The Global Human Capital Trends Report, 2016." http://dupress.com/periodical/human-capital-trends/.

Edelman. "2014 Edelman Trust Barometer: Annual Global Survey." http://www.edelman.com/insights/intellectual-property/2014-edelman-trust-barometer/.

Edelman. "2016 Edelman Trust Barometer: Annual Global Survey." http://www.edelman.com/insights/intellectual-property/2016-edelman-trust-barometer/.

Egon Zehender International and McKinsey & Company. "Return on Leadership—Competencies that Generate Growth." https://www.mckinsey.de/sites/mck_files/files/Return%20on%20Leadership.pdf.

Feeney, Nolan. "Millennials Now Largest Generation in the U.S. Workforce." *Time*, May 11, 2015. http://time.com/3854518/millennials-labor-force.

Gallup. "Employee Engagement Is Stagnant in U.S.," January 13, 2016. http://www.gallup.com/poll/188144/employee-engagement-stagnant-2015.aspx.

Gallup. "State of the American Manager: Analytics and Advice for Leaders," April 2015. http://www.gallup.com/services/182138/state-american-manager.aspx.

Interact. "New Interact Report: Many Leaders Shrink from Straight Talk with Employees." Harris Poll. February 2015. http://www.interactauthentically.com/new-interact-report-many-leaders-shrink-from-straight-talk-with-employees/.

Kallestad, Brent. "2 out of 5 Bosses Don't Keep Word." *LiveScience.com*, January 7, 2007. http://www.livescience.com/9488-study-2-5-bosses-word.html.

Matuson, Roberta Chinsky. *Suddenly in Charge: Managing Up, Managing Down, Succeeding All Around*. Boston: Nicholas Brealey, 2011.

Smith, Ray A. "Why Dressing for Success Leads to Success," *Wall Street Journal*, February 21, 2016. http://www.wsj.com/articles/why-dressing-for-success-leads-to-success-1456110340.

TinyPulse. "New Year Employee Report." https://www.tinypulse.com/landing-page/2015-new-year-employee-report.

Index

planner 132; poor 133; review 34, 39, 55, 64, 104; underwhelming 110–1
Jobs, Steve 9

Kallan, Henry 20, 64–5
Kaplowitz, Marla 114–16
keeping great employees 118–29; leaving speech 119–20; what workers expect from their leaders 120–7
Kenary, Dan 30, 69, 169
Kennedy, Ted 102
Kutaragi, Ken 56–7

lack of: aptitude for job 17, 34; attention 37–8; backbone 39; compassion 136–7; control over work 56–7; enthusiasm 168; feedback 39; passion 34–5; performance 134; trust 63–4
Leondakis, Niki 28, 160
leaving 52, 100, 119–20; costs 40; Gravitational Pull Exercise #10 129
"The Leaving Speech" 119–20
LinkedIn 29, 77, 85, 115, 156, 159
loss-of-productivity costs 42
Lyons, Amy 101–2

magnetic connection principle 19–31; assessing happiness in and with your business 24–5; being social 27–8; beyond happiness 29; boldness 29; common feedback mistakes 25–6; consistency 29; counterattack 26; employees as business owners 30–1; give more than you take 29; Gravitational Pull Exercise #2 31; making the simple complicated 27; social channels are not equal 28; soliciting feedback infrequently 26; unsolicited feedback reaction 26; what to do when the problem is you 25; why money can't buy love or employee happiness 21–2; WOW (Word of Wonderfulness) factor 22–4, 31
magnetic leader 7–18; assessing your current leaders 14–15; better hires, faster, 10–1; corporate growth 13–14; customer satisfaction 12,

29, 138; definition 7; employee commitment and staff productivity 11; Gravitational Pull Exercise #1 18; increased innovation 12; market leadership 1, 13; power 10; reduction in costly employee turnover 11–12; repeat business and referrals 12–13, 20; self-assessment 15–16; traits 7–10; what you need to know when promoting leaders 16–18
Magnetism Equation 141–50; delightful truth about delighting customers 143–4; everyone gets a vote 149–50; everyone's a critic 148–9; forgiving customers 145; Gravitational Pull Exercise #12 150; happier and more productive employees and customers 146–7; how to rewrite your story 150; magnetic leadership + incredible customer service = explosive growth 142–3; nonstop referrals 144–5; profits and possibilities 148; reduced stress 147; reduction in customer acquisition cost 145–6; revenue 147
management by numbers 39
Mandela, Nelson 8
market leadership 1, 13
Matuson, Roberta Chinsky: "How to Create a Solar System of Talent" 118; *Suddenly in Charge* 2; *Talent Magnetism* 40
McClafferty, Sharon 119
McDonnell, Eileen 63, 95
McKinsey & Company (*Return on Leadership*) 13
MEC North America 114
millennials 32–3, 37, 50–1, 55, 66, 93, 169; *The Deloitte Millennial Survey* 57
miserable employees 2, 21
morale 42, 54

networking 83, 87, 90–1, 124, 157, 160
Nixon, Rob 9–10, 69, 76, 119–20, 150
nonstick leadership 32–44; costs of person leaving 40; disengaged leadership of epidemic proportions 33–4; employee turnover true cost 39–40; failure to live up to promises 35; failure to offer opportunity 37;